The Law of Attraction& Manifestations for Happiness Love& Money

33+ Guided Meditations, Hypnosis, Affirmations- Manifesting Desires- Health, Wealth& Abundance Even During Deep Sleep

Table of Contents

Introduction

We believe in the law of gravity because we see it in action every day. We recognize the laws of physics because we can measure and test them. We understand that two like magnets repel each other while two opposite magnets attract each other. In all honesty, nature has a lot of laws; some we see in action every day and some we barely know about. However, all of nature's laws have one thing in common, they work perfectly every time.

The law of attraction is a law of nature and just like every other law of the universe, it works perfectly every time. So why do we not see people receiving their desires each day? How come people struggle every day to reach their goals and experience their life's desires? Well, the answer is simple. The law of attraction is not driven by our thoughts or utterances. The law of attraction is influenced by the powerful subconscious energy that exists beneath the surface of our conscious awareness. Even if all you ever have are positive thoughts, if your subconscious energy is not aligned with the things you want to manifest, the law of attraction cannot work for you.

So what is the answer to tapping into this infinite wealth of energy to manifest abundance, wealth, and even the love of your life? The key is to tap into your subconscious energy and reset it to reflect the things you want to manifest. You must think and believe that you are wealthy to manifest wealth. You must think and believe you are worthy of love to receive love. Everything you want to manifest must come from the belief you hold in your subconscious, become entrenched in your mind before it can manifest into reality.

If you have been looking for a way to use the powerful law of attraction to manifest wealth, abundance, good health and your desires, the insights in this book are meant for you. In the following chapters, we explore how you can use meditation to tap into the powerful energy of the universe to manifest your desires. In the first part of the book, we will show you how to tap into your subconscious energy to create the positivity you need to attract positive outcomes.

This book is for anyone who is struggling to manifest their goals, achieve abundance or

The thoughts on the surface, or the ones you are consciously aware of, are only a product of the subconscious mind that you may not always be aware of. Think of your subconscious as your MacBook's RAM. This RAM quietly runs hundreds of background processes while on your screen you may only be browsing Facebook. The heavy work is taking part in the background and what appears on the surface is only a small fraction of what is going on in your mind.

Once you understand that your subconscious mind is the store of your life's energy then you can utilize the power of meditation to manifest all your dreams and goals. It is not enough to just have positive thoughts but you must delve deeper into the subconscious and change the energy that directs your thoughts. All your deep-seated emotions, habits, experiences and beliefs are stored in your subconscious. Meditation allows you to get into these deeper layers and change your thoughts and energy from the inside out.

As we begin our meditations, realize that it is through the mindfulness of meditation that you can train your mind to focus on the things you want to manifest. The things you are able to bring forth into your life are the ones that you give the most focus to. When you tap deep into your subconscious mind you can train your mind to focus on the things you want to manifest. If most of your subconscious energy is dedicated to your fears, self-limiting beliefs or the things you do not want, then it is not possible to attract the things that you want.

Use meditation as the tool to take charge of your subconscious energy and harness this energy to attract all the things you have ever wanted. Meditation will help you to dig down into the depths of your subconscious and access your mind power in all its fullness. Session by session your level of consciousness and awareness will increase making it easier to direct your energy to manifesting your desires. Naturally, we will start this session with meditations that allow you to delve deep into your subconscious.

Meditation for Tapping Your Subconscious Mind - 25 minutes

This meditation will help you to release subconscious blockages and overcome negative mind blocks.

Duration – 25 minutes

Please start by sitting in a comfortable position in a quiet room free of distractions.

Close your eyes and turn your mind inwards. Shut down all external input. Focus your mind and all your awareness on your breathing.

Feel the breath entering then living your body. Inhale deeply and exhale slowly.

As you continue with the deep breathing, feel your whole body. Start from the top of your head and work your downwards.

Feel the arch of your spine, the curves of your hips all the way down to your toes.

Continue with the deep breathing as you become aware of every part of your body. Inhale deeply and exhale slowly.

As you continue with deep breathing let everything you are feeling rise to the surface. Allow the feelings that reflect what is going on in your life at the moment to rise to the surface. Allow yourself to feel these feelings and thoughts without judgement.

Feel the innermost fears that you are too afraid to voice. Feel the hurts that you keep holding back. Open your mind completely to everything that you keep buried under the surface. Let it all come to the surface.

Acknowledge these feelings and let them wash over you.

Now take a deep breath in through the nose to a count of 6. Hold the breath and then exhale slowly through your mouth.

Take another deep breath in through your nose to a count of 6. Hold the breath and exhale slowly through your mouth.

As you exhale, feel the negative emotions start to leave your body. Release them with every breath you exhale.

Release the fear, the anger, the hurt, the regret, and all the other negative emotions weighing you down.

Feel yourself getting lighter with every negative emotion or thought that you cut loose.

Keep breathing in deeply and exhaling slowly as you free yourself from all the negative thoughts and emotions. Let them all out. Feel yourself getting lighter and more grounded with every exhale.

Allow everything that is weighing you down to leave your body with every exhale. The worries, the regrets, the hurt, the self-doubt; feel them leave your body and see them floating away from you.

Visualize and start to feel the warm rays of the sun on your face every time you exhale and release negative emotions. Feel the warmth of the sun on your face and a soft breeze gently caressing your skin.

Lean into this light and feel yourself become bathed in it.

Gradually allow your breathing to return to its natural rhythm. As you do so keep feeling the warm rays of the sun bathing you in golden light and a fresh breeze caressing your face.

Now take your right hand and place it above your chest.

Repeat this mantra:

I am enough. Today I am happy. Today I am capable. Today I am worthy.

As you say these words visualize the golden light above your head. Feel this light bathing every part of your body from your head to your toes. Give yourself up to the golden light and bask in it.

Repeat the mantra:

I am enough. Today I am happy. Today I am capable. Today I am worthy.

Now visualize your body bathed in the golden light and feel the light start to permeate your being. Let the light in and feel it spread throughout your being. Revel in it and open yourself up to it completely.

Repeat the mantra:

I am enough. Today I am happy. Today I am capable. Today I am worthy.

Now visualize your body as the source of the radiant golden light. Let this light surround you and form an aura of protection all around you.

Breathe in deeply and exhale slowly. Allow yourself to luxuriate in the light, feel it inside you and see it all around you.

You are radiating the light from deep within. Become one with the light.

Repeat the mantra

I am enough. Today I am happy. Today I am capable. Today I am worthy.

Take a deep breath. Hold it and then exhale slowly. Slowly bring your awareness back to the present. When you feel ready you can open your eyes.

This guided meditation is now complete.

Meditation to Let the Universe Guide You - 25 minutes

This meditation is to help you let the universe guide you. It will help you trust your journey and free yourself from constant worry and fear. One of the biggest blocks that keep us away from the things that we want to manifest is the constant need for control. When you are not one with the universe, you will always feel like you are rowing uphill.

If you can let go of the constant stress and worry, the universe will guide you to the things you really want. This state of being is trust and surrender in the purest form. You can repeat this meditation every time you start to feel overwhelmed, doubtful, or disconnected from the present.

So let us get into the meditation.

Duration: 25 minutes

Find a quiet space with minimal distractions for this meditation. You can do it outdoors if possible in a nice quiet spot or indoors.

We will be doing this meditation barefoot so start by taking off your shoes.

Now stand in a comfortable position with your legs and arms in a relaxed stance.

Gently close your eyes and as you do that shut everything else but the awareness of your breathing.

Inhale deeply through your nose then exhale slowly through your mouth.

As you continue to take deep breaths, focus on the feeling of the ground beneath your feet. Bring your awareness to the ground beneath your feet. Focus on feeling grounded and connected to the earth beneath your feet.

Continue with the deep breathing with your mind and awareness focused on the connection between your feet and the ground beneath.

Feel the energy rising up from the ground into your body. Continue to breathe in deeply as you focus on feeling more grounded and connected to the earth through the ground that you are standing on.

Breathe in and feel your body relax, knowing that there is something beneath you holding you up. Feel the connection between your feet and the ground.

Keep taking deep breaths and exhaling slowly allowing your body to sink more and more into a relaxed state.

Now put your hands gently over your heart and take another deep breath in followed by a slow exhale.

Slowly bring your awareness to the top of your head. As you focus your awareness on this part of your body, visualize a warm glow on your forehead. Visualize this glow as a ray that is bathing you in its light and energy.

As the glow lights up your forehead, you start to feel lighter and more relaxed. Now slowly move your awareness down to your cheeks and your neck. As your awareness shifts downwards, let the glow follow suit.

Visualize the ray of light traveling down your body slowly. From the top of your head, down to your chest, your abdomen, your hips, your legs and finally your feet.

Visualize this ray loosening up every part of your body as it travels down. Your head feels lighter, your neck and shoulders are more relaxed.

Let the light relax all your muscles and feel the clean and invigorating energy emanating from the ray of light.

Bask in its glow and feel the heaviness slowly leave your body bit by bit.

You are lighter now, nothing is weighing you down and you are keenly aware of the ground beneath your feet.

You are present in the moment and all that matters is the here and now. Everything that you do not serve you is leaving your body and you feel lighter and lighter.

As you visualize the ray of light traveling all the way down to your feet, take a deep breath and slowly exhale.

Bring your awareness to your right foot and then the left feet that are now bathed in a warm glowing light.

Feel your feet get lighter as negative energy is released from your body to the ground beneath you.

Visualize the fears, the worries, the regrets all flowing out of you and being soaked up into the ground beneath you.

Start to feel lighter as all the negative energy drains downwards into the ground. You are now fully bathed in the warm glow of the ray of light. It is surrounding you and you feel relaxed and at peace.

In this moment, think of your happy place. See it in vivid detail. Feel yourself in this place where nothing and no one can hurt you. Look around you, listen to the sounds and immerse yourself in the experience. You feel at home here, you are safe, you are happy, you are at peace.

Breathe in deeply and feel connected to everything you see around you. Notice the sensations that you are feeling now, look around and observe the things that are surrounding you. This is where you belong, your inner sanctuary.

Visualize yourself walking around in this happy place. Your step is confident and you feel calm and at peace with yourself. Immerse yourself fully in this vision. You see everything that you want and everything that you need. It's all there for you.

As you let yourself soak everything in, repeat this mantra:

Everything I want is within my reach. I already have everything I need. I am one with the universe.

Take a deep breath and again savor your sanctuary and let yourself feel the freedom and peace of having all the things you ever wanted.

Repeat the mantra:

Everything I want is within my reach. I already have everything I need. I am one with the universe.

Inhale deeply and exhale slowly.

Now slowly start to bring your awareness back to the present. Lower your arms from your heart and let them fall back gently to your sides.

Take a deep breath in then gradually allow your breathing to return to normal.

Slowly open your eyes.

This meditation is now complete.

Shifting Consciousness -15 minutes

For most people, the problem is not in not knowing what they want but rather in not knowing how to shift focus from what they do not want. The law of attraction helps you manifest the things that you focus on most. So if you constantly focus on the things you do not want, you will keep manifesting them. The trick, therefore, is to learn to shift your consciousness from what you are trying to avoid or get away from to what you want. It is more important to know what you want rather than what you do not want.

So, if you struggle with keeping your mind on the things that you should be focusing on. This meditation will help you in shifting consciousness to the things you want to manifest.

Let us start the meditation

Duration:15 minutes

Settle into a comfortable position, you can choose to sit or lie down in a quiet room free of distractions.

Eyes closed, place your right hand over your diaphragm, or the area above your navel. Allow yourself to relax and empty your mind of all thoughts.

Now inhale deeply through your nose and exhale slowly through your mouth. Bring your awareness to the rising and falling of your diaphragm as you breathe in and out.

Feel your chest rise as you inhale and feel it fall as you exhale.

Allow yourself to sink deeper into relaxation as you continue to inhale deeply and exhale slowly.

Feel the heaviness of your body begin to lift and feel yourself start to connect deeply with your emotions.

Think of the things that you are grateful for on this day. Your life, your health, your family and all the other things that make your life worth living.

Focus only on the things that make you happy and express gratitude for them.

Repeat this mantra slowly:

I am grateful for my life. I am grateful for everything in my life. I am grateful for this moment.

Continue to take deep breaths while keeping your focus on all the things that you have in your life.

Repeat the mantra:

I am grateful for my life. I am grateful for everything in my life. I am grateful for this moment.

See everything that you are grateful for clearly in your mind. If it is your spouse or your children, see their faces clearly in your mind as you voice your gratitude for them.

If you are grateful for your job see it vividly as you express your gratitude. Everything that you are grateful for, see it, feel it and allow yourself to be connected to all your blessings.

Repeat the mantra:

I am grateful for my life. I am grateful for everything in my life. I am grateful for this moment.

Continue to take deep breaths and feel the air as it enters your body when you inhale and feel it leave your body as you exhale.

With every exhale you feel lighter and more at ease with yourself.

As you continue to ease yourself into deep relaxation, repeat this affirmation:

I will step forward with love and confidence. I am moving forward with courage and grace.

Take a deep breath and exhale slowly through your mouth. Repeat the affirmation:

I will step forward with love and confidence. I am moving forward with courage and grace

As you say this affirmation feel yourself get a fresh burst of confidence as you breathe in. Let this positive energy infuse you from your head to your toe.

Feel it all over you like a soft warm blanket shielding you from the cold.

Repeat the affirmation:

I will step forward with love and confidence. I am moving forward with courage and grace.

Breathe in deeply and again feel the positive energy all around you.

Slowly open your eyes and allow your breathing to go back to normal.

This meditation is now complete.

The Science of a Positive Attitude – 15 minutes

Manifestation relies on your own thoughts and beliefs to bring into reality the things you desire the most. In this way, your thoughts become self-fulfilling prophecies that create the blueprint from which your outcomes are drawn. That is why cultivating positivity is an intrinsic part of the law of attraction and manifesting your desires.

Positive thoughts create the positive energy that you need to attract positive things into your life. That is why it is crucial to bring more awareness into the kind of energy you are putting out into the world. This is the energy that shapes your reality. To help you harness the power of positivity to manifest your desires, this guided meditation will help you train your mind to embrace positivity.

Let us start the meditation.

Duration 15 minutes

Start by finding a comfortable sitting position.

Close your eyes and let your mind and body relax. Shut out all external input and bring your awareness to your inner self.

Take deep breaths and focus on being present in the moment.

Take your time to become aware of every part of your body. Start from the top of your head and work your way down to the tips of your toes.

Take a deep breath to a count of 6, then exhale slowly through your mouth

Bring your awareness to what you are feeling and thinking in the moment. Become aware of your emotions and open yourself up to them.

Continue to take deep breaths, followed by a slow exhale through your mouth.

Now just focus on the rise and fall of your chest

Keeping your eyes closed, listen to my voice as I start to count down from ten to one.

Continue to breathe deeply in that relaxed state

When I say the number 10 I want you to visualize yourself at the top of a small staircase.

As you stand at the top, you can see the bottom of the staircase, where you can see the

most comfortable bed you have ever seen.

The bed looks fresh and inviting with fluffy pillows just waiting for you to get on the bed

As I begin to count down, take a step down the staircase to the divine bed that is waiting for you at the bottom.

With each step that you take, you will feel more relaxed and with each step, you will enter a deeper level of relaxation.

10. You are at the top of the staircase. Now take one step down and feel yourself sink deeper

into relaxation. Breathe in slowly and exhale slowly

9. Take the next step down and as you do see the bed at the bottom get even closer.

8. Another step, you are becoming more limp and loose.

7. Your eyes are getting heavier and heavier.

6. Your whole body is relaxed and the bed is so close now.

5. All the tension in your muscles is slowly easing up.

4. The bottom of the staircase is even closer and you are completely relaxed now.

3. Only two more steps to go now.

2. Take a deep breath and slowly exhale through your mouth.

1. Take the last step and feel yourself sinking into that comfortable bed. Feel the soft covers caress your skin as you lay down on the bed. Feel the comfort of the fluffy pillows underneath your head.

Relax completely and continue to take deep breaths and exhale slowly through your mouth

Now open your mind up completely and see all the things you want to attract and manifest in your life.

See the career that you want, see yourself sitting in that corner office and being the best version of yourself possible.

Visualize yourself sitting behind your desk doing exactly what you have always wanted to do. You are there in that moment, feel it. Look around you. Immerse yourself in it.

Take a deep breath and exhale slowly

Now you can see the family or partner that you have always wanted. See yourself in this role, surrounded by the people you love. Hear their laughter, see their smiles, feel their touch. Immerse yourself in the moment. Reach out and touch. Feel it

Take a deep breath and exhale slowly

Visualize yourself in the prime of health, with the body you have always wanted, in great health and feeling great. Feel the energy in your body, giving you the strength to face anything.

Take a deep breath and exhale slowly

At this point visualize anything else that you want to manifest in yourself. Do not just think about it. Feel it, touch it, immerse yourself in the experience.

Take a deep breath and exhale slowly

As you continue to lie on the divine bed keep bringing to the surface all the things that you want. Feel yourself moving toward them.

Now you can remain in this mindful state of relaxation for as long as you want.

Slowly open your eyes and bring your awareness back to the present.

This meditation is now complete.

Chapter 2: Attract Happiness

Stress and worry are usually a sign that you are not in vibrational alignment with what you would like to manifest. When you are constantly weighed down by negative energy you keep attracting the very things that you worry about. That is why a positive mindset is one of the core elements for manifesting the things you want. If you put out positive energy into the world you will attract joy and abundance.

When you want happiness and abundance you have to actively choose positivity over negativity. You cannot wait until everything works out to be happy. In fact, happiness and living your life in joy and gratitude is what will make it possible for things to work out. However, being positive and finding joy in your life are things you have to actively cultivate. This means using meditation to reset your energy every time you feel weighed down by stress and anxiety.

So, for these next sessions, we will go through meditations to help you find your joy in any circumstances. This will help you align your inner energy with the things you want to manifest. Think of the universe as a kind of mirror that is simply reflecting back what you are putting out. This way you can be more aware of your energy and make a conscious effort to choose joy.

Free Yourself from Anxiety, Stress, and Worry – 20 minutes

This meditation will help you calm an overactive mind and shift your energy from negative emotions and thoughts to a feeling of inner peace and calmness.

Let's get started.

Duration 20 mins

I invite you to make yourself comfortable. You can sit or lie down in a quiet room free of distractions.

We will start this meditation with your eyes open. With a soft gaze focus your line of vision on one point in front of you. This can be a spot on the floor or the wall in front of you. Just find something that draws your attention.

Focus all your attention on this single spot and allow everything else to fade into the background.

Take everything in from this single spot. Notice the color, the textures and notice every single detail about it. Take your time and simply examine this spot.

Now slowly broaden your focus from that single point and expand your focus outward like a camera lens widening.

Again with relaxed awareness, notice every little detail in your expanded view. Notice the color, the texture, and anything else that falls within your line of vision. Take in the details slowly.

Now slowly narrow your vision back down to the original point you had focused on earlier. At this point, as you narrow down your line of vision you are letting everything else fade into the background.

As your focus continues to narrow down, keep making the point of focus smaller and smaller until you gradually close your eyes.

With your eyes closed now, allow your awareness and focus to turn inward.

As you begin to look inside and settle physically, start with three deep breaths in through your nose and followed by a slow exhale through your mouth.

Embrace the feeling of calmness that engulfs you as you continue to take deep breaths.

Now begin to count to 5 as you breathe in then as you breathe out count to 6. With every exhale release any emotional stress and tension in your body. Feel it leave your body as you exhale.

Repeat this breathing cycle five times, each time focusing on releasing anything that is weighing you down. Let it go, and feel the calmness enter your body with every breath you inhale.

Become aware of your physical experience as you continue deep breathing. Notice first the palms of your hands and focus on the energy there. Perhaps you feel this as a warmth or tingling sensation.

Notice how by simply moving your awareness to this part of your body you also feel the energy go where your focus is.

You have the ability to move energy and move a positive sensation within you similar to broadening your visual focus from a single point.

Begin to widen the experience of your sensations by moving your awareness from the palms of your hands to your entire body. Feel your body awaken as you move your consciousness from one part of your body to the rest of your body. Your arms, your legs, your face, your feet.

Feel the energy moving within and you let your attention drift through the sensations in your body without directing it and without judging what you find. Simply allow your focus to tune into the sensations of your body right in this moment.

You are in the present and living in the space between your thoughts when your mind is. You are fully attentive to the sensations of your body.

Between your thoughts, in this space is where you can experience peace and calm

As I mention each part of your body, let your focus and awareness move to that part releasing any tension you feel in that area.

Become aware of your feet. Focus on them and simply relax this part of your body. Slowly move your awareness from your feet and up into your lower legs. Release any tightness in this area and allow it to relax completely as you continue to raise your awareness to your thighs.

Find a sense of ease in your thighs and hips as you let go completely. Then gradually bring your awareness up feeling the arch of your spine your abdomen and your chest. Take a deep breath and allow your upper body to relax completely.

Moving your attention upward feel any tension from your neck relax. Feel any tightness in your jaw and allow it to unclench as every part of your body eases deeper into relaxation.

Feel the small muscles of your cheeks eyes and forehead soften. Now your whole body feels light and relaxed and you feel grounded in the present.

Let your mind and body go deeper into this relaxed state

Now that you are fully relaxed you can begin the inward inquiry process by becoming aware of your emotions.

Experience all your emotions in this present moment without trying to change anything. Let your thoughts come and go. There is no need to attach to them or follow them.

Imagine your thoughts and feelings are flowing like a river and as they leave, you release them and allow fresh clean water to come in.

If you find your mind attaching to a negative thought or emotion, guide yourself back to the present by bringing your awareness back to your body, your breathing, and the sensations in your body.

Begin to deepen your breathing once more and embrace the inner peace and feeling of being present in the moment.

Slowly start to reactivate each part of your body from its relaxed state and feel gentle calming energy flowing into you as you ease yourself back to your normal breathing rhythm.

Now open your eyes slowly and take this calm energy with you as you go on with your day.

This guided meditation is now complete.

Happiness Visualization Technique – 10 minutes

This happiness visualization technique is meant to help you consciously shift your thoughts to a place of happiness and safety whenever you start to feel overwhelmed.

Let us get started.

Duration 10 minutes

Make sure that you are in a quiet space sitting comfortably or lying down

Focus on how you are feeling right now both physically and mentally.

Take a deep breath and repeat quietly in your mind:

I am ready to relax. I am ready to still my mind.

Now take another deep breath nice and slow. Feel your lungs expand and your chest rise.

Pull your breath right down into your belly and then exhale slowly.

You are safe, you are comfortable, you are beginning to relax.

I want you to focus your mind on your heart and imagine a ball of bright green light in the center of your chest

With every breath you take, this ball of light shines brighter and grows bigger

Take another deep breath make sure that you fill your lungs completely.

Repeat quietly in your mind:

I am strong and confident. I am loved just as I am. I am safe.

Continue to breathe slowly and deeply. Feel the flow of air as it moves gently through your body.

Every time you exhale feel any pent-up emotions, stress or anxiety leave your body.

You are safe, you are comfortable, you are relaxed.

Now, I want you to focus your mind on your solar plexus, the area just below your ribs and imagine a ball of bright yellow light in this area.

With every deep breath you take, the light grows bigger and brighter opening your solar plexus chakra to receive more light and love.

You feel strong and confident.

Now take another deep breath and pull the air right down into your solar plexus repeat as you repeat quietly in your mind:

I am strong and confident. I am loved just as I am. I am safe.

Breathe in deeply and with every breath feel your body get filled with confidence and strength. Repeat quietly in your mind:

I am strong and confident. I am loved just as I am. I am safe.

Allow your muscles to ease and soften. Relax your entire body and feel your shoulders and back lose any tension in the muscles.

As your body sinks deeper into relaxation your heart is being filled with a warm loving glow.

Continuing to take deep breaths, repeat quietly in your mind:

I am strong and confident. I am loved just as I am. I am safe.

You can feel a healing warmth spread slowly through your heart. Your mind and body feel lighter your emotions feel lighter you feel lighter.

Now gently stretch your arms and legs. Lift your arms above your head and gently stretch your back.

Take as much time as you need in this relaxed pose and just know that when you open your eyes you will feel refreshed, strong and confident.

Open your eyes when you are ready and slowly bring your awareness back to the present.

This visualization technique is now complete.

Confidence & Self-Esteem Meditation – 20 minutes

When you are full of self-doubt and limiting beliefs, you can only manifest your deepest fears. In times when your thoughts are clouded with self-judgment, the path to things you want to attract becomes blurred. It is only when you can reset your subconscious to have self-belief and self-love that you can truly begin to attract all the things that you deserve.

In this session, I want to guide you on how to bring back your thoughts to a place of self-love and confidence. This will help you in consciously creating the positive vibrational energy that you need to keep attracting happiness and abundance.

Let's get started.

Duration 20 minutes

Make yourself comfortable in a quiet room that is free of distractions. You can sit or lie down for this meditation.

Close your eyes if you like and gradually settle into a relaxed state with your mind only focused on your breathing and the feel of every breath as it enters and leaves your body.

Place your hands over your chest to bring your awareness to your heart and make the physical connection inward.

As you breathe in, imagine that you are breathing in light, love and peace into your heart.

In your mind see it as a bright glowing light that fills your heart and spreads warmth throughout your body.

As you continue to relax deeper and deeper, set the intention to open your heart today and to welcome in love and light.

With every breath in, open yourself up to receiving the loving energy of the world around you and with every breath out radiate that love outward.

See and feel this warm glowing energy entering your body and filling it up and then radiating that energy outward all around you.

Allow this light of love to ground your energy and protect you. Let go of resistance, let go of the tendency to force outcomes, let go of the need for control. Surrender yourself to this new healing and protective energy.

Feel yourself soften and let go with a relaxed awareness as you continue to feel the light radiating from you and protecting you in a safe space.

Now bring your awareness to each and every part of your body feeling the relaxing energy infuse every part of your being from the top of your head to the soles of your feet. You are completely bathed in this loving glow now and you are radiating it into the world in soft waves.

Now that you are in a safe and comfortable state of relaxation, take a deep breath and repeat quietly to yourself:

I am worthy of love. I am worthy of happiness. I am worthy of success.

Continue to feel the warm glow of light bathing you in its warmth and protection. Inhale slowly and deeply and exhale slowly through your mouth.

Repeat quietly to yourself:

I am worthy of love. I am worthy of happiness. I am worthy of success.

You are deeply relaxed and you feel any self-doubt and stress melting away. Your mind is completely relaxed and you have let go of any resistance. You are a source of light radiating a warm glow outwards.

Repeat quietly to yourself:

I am worthy of love. I am worthy of happiness. I am worthy of success.

Feel yourself connecting with your inner glow. Allow yourself to be drawn into the warmth of the light that is now illuminating every part of your being.

Let this light replace any darkness, fear, or doubts. You are enough. You have everything you need to be who you want to be. You are sufficient.

Repeat quietly to yourself. I am worthy of love. I am worthy of happiness. I am worthy of success.

Now take a deep breath and exhale slowly through your mouth.

Slowly bring your attention back to your physical body and your breathing. Gradually bring your awareness back to the present and let yourself soak in the feeling of self-love and acceptance you are feeling in this moment.

You may now open your eyes.

This guided meditation is now complete.

Gratitude is the Key – 10 minutes

One of the easiest ways to attract happiness and live positively is by being grateful. So often we get so caught up in what we want that we overlook what we already have. Yet if you could learn to appreciate what you already have in your life, it will be much easier to attract abundance and joy.

This meditation will help you train your mind to appreciate and be thankful for what you already have. By so doing you will reset your subconscious filter to project the happiness and positivity you need to manifest your deepest desires.

Let's get started.

Duration: 10 minutes

Start by sitting in a comfortable position. Now gently close your eyes and place both of your hands on your chest above your heart.

Relax your whole body and take a deep breath slowly inhaling through your nose, then exhaling through your mouth

Let everything else fade to the background as you bring your awareness and concentration to the fall and rise of your chest as you breathe in and out.

Feel your body sink deeper into relaxation as you continue to inhale deeply and exhale slowly.

Now think about the people in your life and think about who you appreciate. See their smile, feel their touch and remember how they make you feel. Embrace that feeling.

See them one by one in great detail. Maybe it is your spouse, your child, a parent, a friend, or all of the above.

Now take a deep breath and visualize yourself hugging them and bring them closer to you. As you continue to visualize them repeat this mantra:

I am thankful for you. I am happy you are in my life. I am a better person because of you.

Now inhale deeply and exhale slowly. As you exhale shift your focus to the things in your life that you are grateful for. A good job, a nice home, your health, anything in your life right now that you appreciate bring your focus to it.

See it in vivid detail. If it is your home, visualize every room, your favorite place in the home, the little treasures that make it home. If it is your career think of all the milestones you have achieved so far. Visualize all the things you love about your job, your home and your possessions.

See those moments that have brought you joy. See the days that you were strong enough to keep it together no matter what was going on. Find the things about yourself that you are grateful for.

Your inner strength. Your empathy. Your loyalty. Your kindness. What abilities do you have that you are grateful for? Name them one by one in your mind and express your gratitude for them.

Repeat this mantra: I am thankful for who I am, I am thankful for all the things I have. I am thankful for this moment.

Soak in this feeling of gratitude and the blissful feeling of knowing that everything you need, you already have.

Feel the love, compassion, and understanding that gratitude brings into your heart. What are the things you have now that you take for granted? How was you life before you had them?

Reflect on all the challenges you have been through? What have you learned? How have you grown? Are you a better person because of them? Did they help you find hidden strengths you did not know you had?

Take a deep breathe and exhale slowly.

Feel the gratitude take root in your mind and in your heart. Relish the blessings and abundance in your life. Right now, where you are, realize that you are already blessed in more ways than you can count.

Now take a deep breath and exhale slowly. As the air fills your lungs acknowledge what a miracle it is just to be alive. Bring your awareness to your body and how alive it feels right now in this relaxed state.

Now raise both hands in the air and open them up wide as if you want to embrace the air around you. As you do this imagine a beautiful white light shining above your head. Let this light fill your whole being with gratitude and love.

Let this light penetrate every cell in your body, every tissue and every organ. As you continue to open yourself to this light, picture yourself traveling into your ideal life, a life in which you have achieved all your dreams.

See the person that you are in that ideal life. You have everything you ever wanted. You are happy, you are confident, you are successful. You are exactly where you want to be. Look around you, where do you live? Who are you with? How do you feel? Yes, see it, feel it, live it and take a moment to absorb it all.

Take a moment to express gratitude for all you have seen in your vision. Then take a deep breath and exhale slowly through your mouth.

Now imagine yourself traveling back to the present. You are now confident that your ideal life is already waiting for you. You no longer need to worry or live your life in resistance. The universe already knows everything you need and it will bring it to pass. All you need to do is trust your journey.

Take another deep breath and exhale slowly. You can now let your arms fall back to your sides.

As your awareness comes back to the moment take another minute to relish the life that you are destined for.

Slowly open your eyes and take this feeling of gratitude and hope with you throughout the day.

This guided meditation is now complete.

Chapter 3: Attracting Wealth & Abundance

Look at your financial situation right now. Do you have the wealth and abundance you desire? If you have been chasing wealth and abundance with no success, it is important to understand that your beliefs about wealth and money are what are shaping your reality. Often people think that it is their reality that shapes their beliefs but actually it is the other way around; your core beliefs shape your outcomes.

To attract wealth and abundance it is important to disrupt any lack consciousness that you may be subconsciously holding on to. A lack consciousness is when you operate from a belief that there is not enough money, resources, opportunity, love and so on. You are always afraid of running out or falling short. This lack consciousness is what blocks your path to manifesting wealth and abundance. When you wish to create more, you must have the ability to focus on what you want and not what you do not want. A lack consciousness keeps you focused on what you do not have and this blocks the path to the manifestation of wealth and abundance.

To help you get past this barrier, the guided meditations in this section are intended to help you develop a wealth consciousness. This wealth consciousness will help to reset your beliefs about wealth and abundance and set you on the path to attracting all the wealth and abundance you have ever desired.

Manifesting Success with Consciousness - 15 minutes

This meditation will help you overcome any lack consciousness you may have and create a positive money mindset. This guided meditation will help you rewire and reset your relationship with money, wealth and abundance.

Let's get started.

Duration 15 minutes.

I invite you to make yourself comfortable in a quiet space free of distractions. Sit in a comfortable chair with your hands resting gently in your lap. Your feet should be squarely planted on the floor.

Now close your eyes and shut everything out by focusing on your breathing. Inhale deeply and feel the air fill your lungs and exhale slowly through your mouth.

Slowly breathe in and breathe out allowing each subsequent breath to become longer slower and deeper.

Your awareness in this moment should be fully focused on your breathing. Release any thoughts that come into your mind.

As you get deeper into a relaxed state now take a moment and think of all the abundance that is in the world. The abundance that surrounds you every day. The trees you see everywhere, the millions of leaves on all those trees.

The abundance of the air that you are breathing, the abundance of the water in the ocean. The abundance of the light radiating from the sun, the abundance of the stars in the sky at night. See all these things clearly in your mind in their vastness and infinite abundance.

You are a part of all this abundance and it is a part of you. You live in an abundant universe and the universe has everything you will ever need.

Now take a moment to create images in your mind of the kind of life you want. See the house that you want to live in. See it in vivid detail, with all the things that you want in that home. Walk through it from room to room and immerse yourself in its abundance.

As you look at this image of the abundance that is waiting for you, start to picture yourself having all the money you need to buy whatever you want. Feel the money in your hand and see yourself buying anything you want, investing in anything you want and never having to worry about money again.

It's all there in your hand already. Bind yourself to it and feel yourself connect with this wealth.

Now imagine living where you want to live, traveling anywhere you have always wanted to go and doing the things you have always wanted to do. Can you see yourself in those places, living your best life? Can you see yourself taking that trip you always wanted, living in that neighborhood you always dreamed of?

Now pick the specific amount of money you would like to make every month. See this number very clearly in your mind. Be very specific about it. As you think about that number see it on your bank statement, see it in form of a check with your name on it.

See yourself with that money already in your account. Relish the feeling of freedom, abundance and security that having that money gives you. Let that feeling permeate every part of you as you feel any worry about lack or financial insecurity slowly melt away.

Everything you want is expanding in your life. Everything in your life is increasing and you are aware that you can easily allow money to flow into your life. You are aware that abundance is within your reach if you only open and embrace it.

Now you also see yourself sharing your abundance. You do not just have abundance but you are sharing your abundance with the people in your life.

As you take your next breath, imagine money being drawn towards you and into your life. As you exhale see yourself exchanging that money for the things you have always desired. See it vividly and feel those things in your hand.

Luxuriate in the image of having them. Embrace that feeling of abundance. Let it permeate your entire being.

Now take a deep breath and exhale slowly through your mouth. Repeat this affirmation:

I love my abundant life. I choose to succeed and prosper in every area of my life. I have abundance and wealth. I have all the wealth I desire.

And now take a minute to simply be grateful for all the abundance flowing into your life this very moment. Feel the freedom, the security and the joy of abundance.

Repeat this affirmation: I love my abundant life. I choose to succeed and prosper in every area of my life. I have abundance and wealth. I have all the wealth I desire.

As you say those words, connect with this abundance and attach yourself to it. You are wealthy, you have abundance, you have all the money you want. Immerse yourself in this feeling of having everything you need.

Now slowly bring your awareness back to the present. Take a deep breath and focus on the sensation of the air filling your lungs, and then exhale slowly. Take another deep breath and slowly open your eyes.

This guided meditation is now complete.

Wealth Visualization Techniques - 10 minutes

When you want to manifest wealth, it is important to keep the following in mind. The key to manifesting the wealth and abundance you want is to always see yourself in the picture and visualize your life exactly as you want it to be. You must first see the things that you want in your mind before you can manifest them into reality.

This wealth visualization technique is a quick and simple meditation that you can do twice or thrice a day to manifest the wealth that you want.

Let's get started.

Duration: 10 minutes.

Sit in a comfortable position. You can sit in a chair or on the floor in a cross-legged posture. Just make sure your body is relaxed.

Start by closing your eyes. To bring your awareness inward, let us concentrate on breathing.

Take a deep breath in through your nose and exhale slowly through your mouth. Now take another deep breath and as you feel the air enter your body let your body sink deeper into relaxation.

In this relaxed state, with your eyes still closed imagine that you are looking towards the center of your forehead. This is the location of the third chakra. This chakra is a powerful manifestation point that will make your visualization even more powerful.

As you focus on this point on your forehead, continue taking deep slow breaths. As your mind gets calmer and more relaxed you will feel more centered.

Now in this relaxed state visualize yourself living in wealth and abundance. Be very detailed in what you see. If it's a new home that you are in, see it in vivid detail. The structure itself, the furniture in it and everything else that you want in that home. See yourself in this beautiful home, living in it with your loved ones.

Immerse yourself completely in the visualization. Touch the fixtures and furniture. Sit in a chair. Walk around the rooms in this home. Become one with it. Experience it.

Continue to visualize the thing you want the most. If it is money. Feel the notes in your hand, crisp and bundled up. See yourself walking to the bank and withdrawing all the money you need. Can you feel the money in your hands? Can you feel the freedom and security of having it?

Whatever it is that you want, see yourself having it. If it is a new car, visualize yourself driving it. Visualize the feel of the steering wheel in your hand, the quiet hum of the engine as you drive and the smell of the interior. See it, touch it, drive it. It is yours, experience it.

Now as you continue to soak up this feeling of abundance repeat this affirmation quietly in your mind.

I am grateful for my money. I am financially free. I make money easily. I always have enough money.

Now take a deep breath as you slowly bring your awareness back to the present. Repeat the afiirmation one more time.

I am grateful for my money. I am financially free. I make money easily. I always have enough money.

Stay with this feeling of abundance and wealth for a minute and allow yourself to keep that feeling with you throughout the day

You can repeat this visualization as often as you want throughout the door to keep you connected to the things you want to manifest.

This guided visualization is now complete.

Creating Opportunity - 15 minutes

If you constantly feel like there are obstacles in your path blocking your abundance and wealth, this meditation will guide you through the mental blocks. Whether you are yearning for your dream job, a business you have always wanted or any other opportunities, resetting your subconscious energy to align with your goals will help you manifest the opportunities you want.

Let us get started.

Duration 15 minutes.

Let us begin by settling down in a comfortable position. You can choose to sit or lie down with your eyes closed for this meditation. Find a quiet room that is free of distractions.

Now let's start by directing your awareness inward and shutting out everything else. Inhale deeply through your nose and exhale slowly through your mouth. Again, inhale deeply, letting the air fill your lungs completely then exhale slowly.

As your mind starts to relax, concentrate on the feeling of the air entering and leaving your body. If any errant thoughts come to mind, simply release them and let them float away.

Bring your awareness to your body starting from the top of your head. As you focus on each part feel it come alive.

Slowly work your way down from your head bringing your awareness to your neck and shoulders. If there is any tension there feel it ease as you continue with the deep breathing.

Now bring your awareness down to your spine and abdomen. Feel the warmth spread from your head downwards as you continue to scan your body. Your back is now comfortable and relaxed and this feeling is spreading down to your legs.

As you continue all the way down to your feet, your whole body is now fully relaxed and you feel light and calm.

Now in this relaxed state visualize yourself walking into your ideal job. See yourself walking through the doors and confidently walking to a bright and beautiful workspace. Feel yourself take a seat in this beautiful office. Look around you and take in your surroundings.

Take your time to explore this space. If it is the business you have always wanted to open. See the sign and branding on the window with your company's name on it. Walk through the doors and see the setup you have always wanted. Touch the furniture, look out the window, what do you see?

Whatever it is that you want to come into your life, see yourself having it now. The job, the business, the promotion, the leadership role. Picture yourself in that role and experience it vividly. You are there right now doing what you have always wanted.

You feel valued and abundant in this space. You are interacting with people in this abundant space.

You are confident in your accomplishments, your skills and your potential. This is who you are. This is the version of yourself that you want to be the most.

Feel the joy of being exactly where you want to be. Bathe in the confidence of knowing you can accomplish anything you want and that every opportunity you crave is opening itself up to you right now in this moment.

Notice how your body feels in this moment. Tune in to your emotions and fill the energy running through your body at this moment when you are in the role you have always wanted. Experience these sensations and radiant energy in your body and your mind.

Now imagine that this energy is vibrating and radiating outwards enveloping your body like a warm cozy blanket. This energy is now surrounding you and now filling your whole room radiating outside into the universe.

Let yourself release this powerful energy into the world and onto the deep space where opportunities are waiting for you to grab them.

See this radiant energy cover and infuse everything around you. Now stay connected to this moment for a little while.

Take a deep breath and begin to release all the concentration and expectations that you have. Simply allow yourself to bask in this positive energy trusting that what you want is going to manifest.

Slowly bring your awareness back to the present and open your eyes.

You can repeat this meditation twice a day to keep your mind open to opportunities.

This guided meditation is now complete.

Wealth Affirmations - 10 minutes

Everything that you want to manifest must first be birthed in your mind. These wealth affirmations are powerful tools to help you manifest abundance and wealth.

Repeat these affirmations every morning for 21 days to tune into the vibrations of wealth and abundance.

Let's get started.

Duration: 10 minutes

I am a money magnet.

I attract money and abundance easily.

I am a money magnet.

Money comes to me easily.

I live abundantly and money serves my highest good.

I am a money magnet.

I have all the money that I need.

I deserve abundance and wealth.

I invite wealth and abundance into my life.

I am getting wealthier each day.

I deserve to prosper.

I open myself up to embrace wealth and abundance.

Money flows into my life easily.

I am a money magnet.

I release my resistance to money.

I release my lack consciousness.

I deserve wealth.

I am wealthy.

I am a money magnet.

Money comes to me easily.

My income continues growing.

My finances are great.

I have all the money that I need.

I am a money magnet.

I am grateful for my wealth and abundance.

I am open to abundance and wealth.

I can feel my financial abundance daily.

I can feel my financial abundance increasing daily

Every day I become wealthier.

Every day my abundance increases.

I am destined to live abundantly.

I am grateful for my wealth.

I am thankful for my abundance.

The universe provides for me.

I will never lack.

I am getting wealthier each day.

Chapter 4: Manifesting Love

We spend a lot of time fighting off the creations of our own minds. In relationships, just like in wealth and abundance, we manifest our deepest beliefs and preconceived notions. This means that unless you can align your subconscious energy with the kind of person you want to attract you will keep struggling to find fulfilling relationships. Our beliefs follow us around like a shadow and they infuse us with whatever energy that we have created. This energy can then either manifest the love and relationships you want or take you further and further away from them.

Love is an integral part of abundant and fulfilling life. If you want to attract your soulmate or healthy relationships, the work starts on the inside before it can manifest on the outside.

For these sessions on attracting love, the guided meditations are intended to help you manifest the person of your dreams and have the relationships you yearn for.

Heart Chakra Activation - 15 minutes

This heart chakra activation meditation will help you open yourself up to love and attract your soulmate. It will help you overcome any self-limiting beliefs you have about love and relationships.

You can practice this meditation before you go to bed or when you wake up in the morning.

Let's get into it.

Duration 15 minutes

Start by sitting in a comfortable position. Your neck and spine should be aligned in a relaxed position.

Now place your hands on your thighs with the palms facing upward ready to receive what the universe has to offer.

In this relaxed stance close your eyes and take a deep breath in through your nose. As you exhale slowly, let your mind clear of all thoughts and distractions. Simply concentrate on your breathing and release any thoughts in your mind.

As you sink deeper into relaxation start to visualize a radiant light surrounding your heart and getting brighter with every breath you take.

You can feel the warm glow of this radiant light all over your chest and the warmth is slowly spreading throughout your body. You are opening yourself up to receive love and making room in your heart for your soulmate.

Feel this warm glow become a vibrant energy that is permeating every part of your body. As you continue to feel this positive energy repeat these affirmations quietly in your mind.

I am attracting my soulmate.

I feel my soulmate is strongly attracted to me.

I believe in my ability to attract my soulmate I feel it within every cell of my body.

My soul mates and I are being drawn closer and closer together each day.

I love being with my soulmate.

My heart is open to receive and give love to my soulmate.

I now attract the perfect partner in my life.

I have more love than I ever thought was possible.

I naturally and effortlessly attract healthy loving relationships into my life.

I am deeply connected to my soulmate.

I'm in the right place at the right time to meet my perfect partner.

I will let my soul and my spirit guide me into my soulmate.

I release everything that is standing in the way of love.

I am attracting my perfect partner.

I am attracting the love of my life.

I've now found the love of my life

I'm extremely grateful for all the love in my life.

I'm so thankful that I have attracted my soulmate.

I attract love and everything that I do.

I'm so grateful for my love life.

True love is my divine birthright and I claim it now.

I opened my heart to myself and I trust that true love will follow and flow through me.

I love myself and I attract loving relationships into my life.

This loving relationship enhances my being and brightens up my life.

I have entirely detached of any outcome and have for trust that my heart will lead me to where I need to go.

The more I love myself the more I love my soulmate.

I am in total acceptance and receive the love my soulmate has for me.

As I relax in this moment, in this very moment I feel this positive love and energy radiate through me and I become one with this love.

I become love. I am love and I attract true love to my life.

Now take a deep breath and slowly start to bring your awareness back to the present.

Take a deep breath in and out. And again, deep breath in and then exhale slowly.

Slowly open your eyes

This guided meditation is now complete.

Affirm Your Belief in Your Soulmate - 15 minutes

If you want to find the perfect partner, you have to be intentional about sending the right energy out into the universe. This meditation will help you affirm your belief in your soulmate and open yourself up to manifesting the partner that you want in your life.

Let us get started.

Duration 15 minutes

For this meditation find a quiet place and sit in a comfortable chair.

Keep your back straight and your shoulders back in a relaxed but upright sitting position. Your feet should be flat on the ground.

Place your hands on your lap with the palm facing upwards as a sign that you are open to receive what the universe has to offer.

Now gently close your eyes and allow yourself to focus on your breath. Inhale deeply making a point to focus on the rise and fall of your chest as you continue to inhale deeply and exhale slowly.

Let the calmness take hold and release any lingering thoughts in your mind. Simply focus on breathing and following the rhythm of your chest as it rises and falls.

With every inhale feel the clean air nourish your body while every exhale releases any resistance to love, any negative thoughts and any negative emotions. Let them all float away as you continue to inhale nourishing energy with every breath you take.

As you continue with the deep breathing, bring your awareness to the energy center of your heart which is at the center of your heart.

Focus all your awareness on this chakra point as you continue to open up your heart and your mind to accept your soulmate.

Now with your heart chakra fully receptive to the universe. Start to visualize yourself seated at the top of a peaceful lush hill. There is nothing but green healthy vegetation as far as the eye can see and you are surrounded by all this beauty and open space.

In this moment you are ready and open to connect with your soulmate. Now in this relaxed beautiful place repeat these affirmations.

I love and accept you. I welcome you in whenever you're ready.

Now take a deep breath, and fill the clean fresh air fill your lungs. Now exhale slowly and as you release the air release with it the need for your soulmate to be here right now. Instead, release this need for attachment trusting that your soulmate will come to you at the right time.

Your journey and your soulmates are intertwined and you are a magnet attracting them to you through the vast expanse surrounding you.

Allow yourself to be open to your soulmate without needing to control the timeline or where it happens. You are patient knowing that your soulmate is coming to you and you are ready to receive them.

Although they are not here with you now, allow yourself to relax into their love just feeling the energetic presence of their love. Notice how it feels to know that they are there. The comfort of knowing that you are going to meet your perfect partner.

Trust and know that even when they are not with you in the physical that you can connect with their energy feel their love and let them feel yours in return. You are connected now and your energies are aligned.

Notice the way you want to feel with them long before you ever are near them physically. You can just love them for wherever they are and whatever they're doing trusting that they will come into your life.

You simply enjoy the fact that you know they are out there. You know you are both going through whatever you need to go through so that you may meet at the perfect timing.

In the next few moments just send appreciation to them wherever they are, whatever they're doing.

Repeat this affirmation.

I love and accept you. I appreciate you. I know we will meet when the timing is right.

Now take this feeling of love, acceptance and appreciation with you and hold on to it until the time is right for your lives to come together.

Take a deep breath and feel the love in your heart as you hold on to the connection you feel to your soulmate.

Slowly bring your awareness back to the present by tuning into the rhythm of your breathing. You can now open your eyes slowly.

This guided meditation is now complete.

Manifest Your Partner, Lover, & Improve Your Relationship - 25 minutes

Sometimes the partner of your dreams is already in your life but your relationship has hit a snag. Or you want to mend a broken relationship. To attract your partner back into your life or heal your relationship, you need to manifest this desire by aligning your subconscious energy with the relationship you want to attract.

Let's get into this healing mediation.

Duration 25 minutes.

For this meditation, you can lie back in a comfortable position. Make sure you are in a quiet room free of any noise or distractions. You can also choose to sit on a comfortable chair or the floor.

If you are sitting up, make sure you are sitting up straight. Pull your chin down to aligning your neck with your spine in an upright but relaxed posture.

Place your palms face upwards by your side if you are lying down or on your lap if you are sitting down. This opens up to connect with the energy around you.

Bring your awareness to how you are feeling in this very moment. Become aware of how you feel, any thoughts running in your mind and how your body feels.

Now begin your cycle of deep breathing that will be our anchor throughout this meditation.

Inhale slowly and deeply through your nose and as you do so feel your mind start to clear. With every exhale you are releasing any errant thoughts and negative emotions.

Inhale deeply and exhale slowly. Inhale deeply and exhale slowly. Inhale deeply and exhale slowly.

As you continue with the deep breathing start to bring your awareness to your body. Start with your feet feeling a tingling sensation there as you focus on them. Now continue to scan upwards and feel this tingling sensation travel slowly up your body.

As you feel the energy spreading throughout your body, let your body relax and feel the energy infuse every part of your body.

Become aware of how your breath keeps you focused and connected with yourself and with the universe.

Your breath is a vehicle between your body and everything that you desire. Trust in the process of your breath.

Inhale deeply and exhale slowly. Inhale deeply and exhale slowly. Inhale deeply and exhale slowly.

Feel your body sink deeper and deeper into relaxation and the radiant energy coursing through your body.

Now set an intention for this meditation. Do you want to mend your relationship? Are you looking for your soulmate? Do you want a healthier relationship? Whatever your intention is be very clear about it.

If your desire is someone in particular, see them in vivid detail. Their face, their smile, their eyes. See them exactly as they are.

Get as clear as possible on what it is you desire.

Focus on your desire and intention. On your next deep inhale, repeat this affirmation:

I deserve this connection.

On your next inhale, repeat this affirmation - I am ready to call this connection into my life.

Now breathe in and repeat this affirmation - I can feel my desire.

As you breathe out repeat this affirmation - I am ready to experience my desire

Inhale deeply and repeat this affirmation - I can see clearly what I want

As you exhale, repeat this affirmation - I know that it is coming toward me

You are now consciously connecting to the powerful energy of the universe. And you are aware that what you seek is also seeking you.

Take a long moment and be grateful knowing that the love you are seeking is also searching for you.

Breathe in the gratitude of this surety. Embrace this feeling and let yourself feel it deeply.

With each grateful breath in, you are becoming a part of everything positive that is working in the universe.

You are calling in your perfect partner and the universe is releasing them to you. Feel them in this moment there with you, connected and sharing in your life. Hold their hand and embrace the feeling of being with the one you desire.

As you experience these feelings, you are bringing your desires closer and closer. You are feeling gratitude. You are feeling joy. You are feeling at peace. You are content.

You and the power of the universe are working together to bring your desire to pass.

Breathe in deeply and exhale slowly. Now visualize your lover or ideal partner moving towards you.

Imagine that you are standing in a giant, sunny field with your soulmate. Visualize them looking at you. See how they loom deep into your eyes and feel them take your hand in theirs. Feel the connection between you two.

Keep deep breathing and anchoring yourself to the present moment.

In this present moment is where your future manifestations are being born. In this present moment, all that you want is beginning to unfold.

Everything you want is already here, in front of you.

Deep breath in, slow exhale. Deep breath in, slow exhale and again a deep breath in followed by a slow exhale.

Now visualize your soulmate and you standing across from you in this sunny, peaceful, quiet field, imagine looking up at the beautiful sky.

As you begin to enjoy the view of the sky a golden light begins descending from the sky above you two.

The golden light begins to move slowly down to where the two of you stand. As you both look up at the light, you feel a sense of true calm and peace inside of your hearts.

This light continues to move toward you and enters your body through the crown of your head. You can both feel this warm glow spreading throughout your body and connecting you to each other. You are now bound by this radiant energy and you are one.

You see each other, full of light, full of connection and strong feelings for each other. The golden light wraps the two of you together, slowly and powerfully circling your bodies. It is bonding you together and healing any hurtful past or heartbreak.

This is a new, fresh start. You are safe and surrounded by the loving energy of the universe.

You see the sense of calm in your partner. You feel calm. You feel peaceful.

Continue with deep breathing and as you do so, bring to the surface all the feelings you long to feel.

You feel loved. You feel wanted. You feel appreciated. You feel like you belong. You feel safe. You are surrounded by your heart's deepest desires.

Stay connected to these feelings and let them permeate your being. You are living these feelings in this moment. Let them infuse you with positive energy and open you up to receive the love you deserve.

Keep visualizing that golden light surrounding the two of you. The light is pulling you together and keeping you connected.

You are one. You are not afraid. You do not doubt. You feel clarity. You do not bring fear into this relationship.

This light that surrounds you is pure, and nothing harmful can enter this energy you are experiencing.

You deserve these feelings, this light, and this person.

Now I want you to bring back your intention that you set at the beginning of the meditation.

Breathe into your intention.

As you visualize this person standing in front of you, imagine what your relationship looks like with them.

How you feel in the relationship, how you are treated, how you treat your partner, how attracted you are to each other.

Let your imagination run wild with future sensual, happy moments with your partner. Imagine what you are looking forward to the most.

Their presence is here with you now, and your longing is being fulfilled. Breathe into your partner's presence and begin to identify why they make you feel happy and fulfilled.

Now breathe in deeply and exhale slowly. Deep breath in, followed by a slow exhale. Breathe in breathe out

As you continue to breathe and dwell in this light, visualize your relationship freeing you from any limiting beliefs about love that you may hold in your mind.

Your relationship is limitless. This relationship will provide the full connection and freedom that you desire.

You and your soulmate are one. You feel strong. You feel secure.

Now with a deep inhale and exhale, start to bring awareness back to your body. Focus on the top of your head and slowly bring your awareness down your neck and shoulders. Now your back, slowly down to your thighs and eventually your feet.

Let your body awaken slowly and as it does so, bring your awareness back to the present by focusing on the rhythm of your breathing.

Now take in a slow deep breath then exhale slowly. Breathe in deeply and exhale slowly through your mouth. One more time, deep breath in, slow exhale.

Now you can open your eyes and take this feeling of love, security and freedom with you throughout the day.

This guided meditation is now complete.

Affirmations to Attract Your

Soulmate and Attract Love -10 minutes

Affirmations help you to set your intentions and make them clear to the universe. This helps you send out the right energy to manifest the things you desire most.

You can repeat these powerful love affirmations before you go to sleep or first thing in the morning.

Let's get started:

Duration: 10 minutes

I radiate loving energy into the universe.

My heart is open to receiving and giving love.

I am a magnet to the love of my dreams.

There are countless opportunities to meet my love.

I trust the universe to send me my ideal.

I am worthy of a relationship filled with mutual respect and love.

I have attracted the most loving person into my life.

I am in the right place and at the right time to attract my soulmate.

I surrender to my soul and intuition to guide me to my soulmate.

I release anything that is blocking love out of my life.

Love is flowing to me and through me at all times

I are destined to be together.

Positive loving energy is growing between my partner and me.

The attraction energy between me and my soulmate grows each day.

I will meet my ideal partner.

I am attracting the partner I desire.

I will find my soulmate and the love that I deserve.

Love is flowing through my spirit and attracting my ideal partner to me.

I am a love magnet and my soulmate is coming towards me.

The soulmate I seek is also seeking me.

My mind and heart are open to receiving and giving love.

My relationship is healthy and happy.

My desires are coming true.

I am surrounded by a loving universe that is releasing love and abundance into my life.

I am aligned with the energy of my soulmate.

The universe is bringing me my perfect partner.

I am grateful for the love that is coming to my life.

I am thankful for my partner.

I release any past hurts and broken relationships.

I am ready to be in a loving and healthy relationship.

My heart and spirit are connected with my soulmate.

My heart is open and I radiate love.

I am sending the perfect energy out into the world and my arms are open to receive love from the universe.

I have the soulmate I desire. I have the love I deserve. I am surrounded by love.

Chapter 5; Manifesting Health & Wellness

If you struggle with chronic health conditions or constant stress and anxiety, meditation is not just a powerful coping technique but can also help to restore your vitality. Meditation helps you to create harmony between your mind and body and use this harmony to manifest good health. Your mind and body are in sync and the energy from your mind can affect your physical health. I am sure you have noticed that you are more prone to infections when you are stressed out or going through turmoil. This is simply because your mental energy affects your physical state.

This mental distress ends up manifesting physically in terms of illnesses, sleep disorders, eating disorders, and a host of other conditions that impact your health negatively. That is why healing often starts from the inside out because your mind and your subconscious energy need to be in the right place to attract good health and vitality. Fortunately, meditation is an effective way to nurture your body and mind back to wellness and enjoy a healthy life.

The guided meditations in this section are intended to help you attract and manifest good health and wellbeing. This includes your mental, spiritual and physical wellbeing. Whether you want to lose weight, overcome chronic stress or cope with an illness, meditation will guide you to a safe and healthy place.

Guided Morning Meditation for a Healthy Body -20 minutes

This guided meditation will help you tap into your body's self-healing mechanism to attract a healthier body.

Let's get started.

Duration: 20 minutes

Start by making yourself comfortable. You can choose to either lay down or sit in a comfortable position in a chair or on the floor.

Now close your eyes gently and begin to block all external input by bringing your awareness to your breathing.

Start by taking a deep breath feeling the air as it enters your body, then taking your time to exhale slowly.

Take another deep breath through your nose, hold it for a moment and then exhale slowly and as you do begin to fill your mind releasing any errant thoughts.

As you continue breathing deeply, you can feel your body start to relax. Tension is leaving your muscles, and you are releasing any negative energy from your body.

With each breathing cycle, allow your mind and body to sink deeper and deeper into relaxation. You feel calm and grounded to the present. Your mind is clear and open and your body feels light and relaxed.

Deep breath in, hold for a while then slowly exhale. As you exhale you are releasing negative thoughts, all feelings of anxiety, all worries and all fears.

As you inhale, you are feeling your body with a positive vibrant energy that is spreading a soothing warmness to every part of your body.

Deep breath in, hold for a while, then exhale slowly through your mouth. You feel peaceful and calm.

Each breath out is freeing you from anxiety, stress and negative thoughts.

Each breath in is cleansing your mind, your spirit and your body. You are filled with healing energy and your body is protected by this energy that is now flowing in you.

Notice how relaxed and calm you feel in this moment and now start to bring awareness to every part of your body.

Start at the top of your head and feel for any aches or pains. As your awareness move to each part, let the healing energy cleanse it and release it from any pain or tension.

Slowly move your attention down to your neck and shoulders. Feel for any tension in your muscles and slowly roll your shoulders back as the healing energy soothes and nourishes this part of your body.

Continue to bring your awareness down to your abdomen and back, slowly arch your spine as you feel the healing energy travel down and ease any aches and pains in this part of your body. Relax your spine back into a comfortable posture and continue to scan your body downwards.

From your upper thighs, feel the healing energy spread a healing warmth in your muscles, knees, calves and finally your feet. Your entire body is now at ease and you have released any tension, pain and discomfort in your body.

Lean into this feeling of wholesome wellness and appreciate how you feel in this moment. Notice how much lighter your body feels and how much clearer your mind is.

Now that your body is completely relaxed, open yourself up to receive healing of your mind and body.

Repeat this affirmation quietly in your mind – I am healthy. I invite healing into my body.

Deep breath in, hold for a while, now exhale slowly through your mouth and repeat this affirmation - I am physically and emotionally connected to an abundant source of healing.

As you repeat these affirmations you can still feel the healing energy within your body and radiating all around you. You are covered in it and it is protecting you from any illness, stress or pain.

Continue with the deep breathing as you scan your body from head to toe, again releasing any tension that you feel in any part of your body by bringing your awareness to it.

Repeat these affirmations:

Every time I think healing thoughts, my body gets healthier.

I treat my body with respect.

I choose food that nourishes every cell in my body.

I choose thoughts that feel like love to me.

I am choosing to get healthy.

I am choosing to be healthy.

I am grateful for my health.

My body is full of healing energy.

I deserve to be healthy.

As you continue to affirm your health you can feel every cell in your body aligning with this positive healing energy. You feel an overwhelming sense of wellness and wholeness.

Immerse yourself fully in this sense of well-being and take another deep healing breath and exhale slowly.

Repeat these affirmations one more time:

Every time I think healing thoughts, my body gets healthier.

I treat my body with respect.

I choose food that nourishes every cell in my body.

I choose thoughts that feel like love to me.

I am choosing to get healthy.

I am choosing to be healthy.

I am grateful for my health.

My body is full of healing energy.

I deserve to be healthy.

Now take a deep breath and as you exhale start to bring your awareness back to the present by focusing on your breathing.

Feel every breath as it enters your body and then exhale slowly noticing how your chest expands and contracts.

You can now gently open your eyes.

This guided meditation is now complete.

You can practice this meditation every night before you go to sleep to relieve your body of the physical and mental stress of the day.

Meditation for Weight Loss - 20 minutes

For those who struggle with weight loss, often the problem starts with an unhealthy relationship with their bodies and with food. If you have self-limiting beliefs about health and weight loss in your mind, these beliefs may be hindering you from manifesting the healthy body that you want. With meditation, you can reset any mental blocks that prevent you from having a healthy relationship with your body and manifest your weight loss goals.

Let us get into the weight loss meditation.

Practice this meditation daily for at least 21 days to start manifesting your weight loss goals.

Duration 20 minutes

For this meditation start by sitting on the floor in a comfortable position with your legs crossed. You can also choose to sit in a comfortable chair with your feet planted firmly on the ground.

Now place your hands on your lap with the palm facing upwards ready to receive from the universe whatever energy you need for your intentions.

Gently close your eyes and as you do so you are going to start taking deep slow breaths in through your nose and exhale slowly through your mouth.

Deep breath in, hold for a while, then exhale slowly.

As you continue with the deep breathing your awareness and focus are on the rhythmic rise and fall of your chest. You are releasing any errant thoughts in your head and focusing your attention simply on the sensation of breathing in and out.

As you breathe in, feel your chest rise as your lungs fill with air and as you exhale, feel your chest relax.

As your continue with the deep breathing, your mind is getting clearer and your body now feels more relaxed.

Now with your eyes still closed, focus on the center of your forehead or your third eye. You want to use this powerful chakra point to reset your mindset about your weight.

To focus on this chakra spot just imagine your eyes are fixed on the center point in the middle of your forehead.

Now with your awareness fully focused on your third eye, you are going to start releasing any unhealthy attachments as you breathe out.

Take a deep breath and as you continue with the deep breathing start to visualize yourself standing in front of a full-length mirror. You can see every inch of your body in this mirror exactly as you are in this moment.

As you look in the mirror next to you is a notepad with the number 10 written on it. This number symbolizes your current weight. Look at this number and then look at yourself in the mirror.

At the next inhale, see yourself flipping the page on the notepad. Now the number on the page is 9. When you look in the mirror you can see that you are starting to lose weight. You feel lighter and your body looks smaller.

Take a deep breath and exhale slowly.

Again, still looking at yourself in the full-length mirror flip to the next page on the notepad. The number on this page is 8. As you see this number look back at the mirror and look at your body. You are even slimmer now and you have lost a little bit more weight.

Notice how much slimmer you look right now. Your body also feels healthier and lighter. As you continue to look at your reflection in the mirror feel the relief and gratitude of knowing that you are losing weight already.

Look in the mirror and if you still want to lose more weight flip to the next page of the notepad. You are now at number 7 and you have lost even more weight. You have a much slimmer body and you feel healthier and stronger.

As you continue to look at your slimmer self, feel the joy of being in a slimmer body. Look at this slimmer version of yourself reflected in the mirror and imagine what you will feel like in this body. Revel in this feeling and connect to this new healthier you.

Notice every little detail of your smaller body. Notice how it looks and how it feels to be in the body you have always wanted.

As you continue to look at your slimmer body, flip to the next page of the notepad. You are now at number 6. With every page you turn, your body gets slimmer and the body you see reflected in the mirror looks better and healthier.

As you continue with this visualization, when the reflection that you see in the mirror is the body that you want to achieve, you can stop flipping the pages.

If the image you see at number 6 is exactly what you want your body to look like, you do not need to flip to the next page. Simply look at your new slimmer self and take in every detail of your slimmer body.

Notice the curve of your hips, your waistline, your abdomen and every other little detail of your body. See it, internalize it and commit to your mind that this is what your body looks like.

If you want to keep losing even more weight you can keep flipping the pages on the notebook until the image that you see in the mirror is exactly the body that you want to manifest.

When you find the perfect image of yourself, let yourself feel the emotional connection with your new slimmer body. See yourself, walking around in this body, dressing this slimmer body and connect with it as deeply as possible.

How does it feel seeing yourself fit and healthy? How liberating is it to let go of the excess weight and live in the body you desire? Notice what you are feeling right now in this moment looking at a slimmer and healthier you in the mirror.

Feel the joy and gratitude of no longer having to feel unhealthy or ashamed of your body. Feel the freedom of knowing you can wear anything you want and do anything you want.

You are healthier, you are slimmer and you look beautiful in this new slimmer body.

You are free of all the excess body weight and free of any unhealthy attachments to food.

As you continue to gaze upon your new slimmer self, bring your left palm up placing it above your heart. Now place your right palm above your left.

With both palms now above your heart, take a deep breath and repeat these affirmations quietly in your mind.

I am joyfully achieving my weight loss goals.

I am losing weight every single day.

I enjoy eating healthy foods.

I eat only when I feel hungry and control how much I eat.

I am becoming fitter and stronger every day.

I can easily reach and maintain my ideal weight.

I love and care for my body.

As you affirm your weight loss intentions stay connected to the image of a slimmer and healthier you. See it in great detail and feel the joy of having that body that is free of excess weight.

Now place your palms back in your lap and take a deep breath followed by a slow exhale through your mouth.

Slowly start to bring yourself back to the present by bringing your awareness to your breathing. Feel your chest rise and fall rhythmically as you breathe in and out.

When you are ready you can now open your eyes.

This guided meditation is now complete.

Healing Meditation for Pain Relief - 10 minutes

For people with painful conditions, this healing meditation is designed to help you activate your body's self-healing mechanism from the inside out. It will help you radiate the healing energy that you need to manifest a pain-free body and a healthier stronger you.

Let's get into it.

Duration 10 minutes

Find a comfortable spot to sit in a quiet and peaceful environment. You can sit on a chair or the floor. Just make sure you are sitting up in an upright but relaxed posture.

Now gently close your eyes and start to shut everything else out apart from the sensation of your breaths. Feel the air as it fills your lungs and then exhale slowly allowing yourself to release any pent-up stress.

As you continue to breathe deeply, start to feel the weight of your body. Your body on the chair or the floor.

Become aware of your body. Your body right here and now. Focus on the muscles and any tense areas as you start to relax them and release any tension with every exhale.

Feel your neck and your shoulders relax. Allow every muscle in your body to soften and let your body sink deeper into relaxation.

Now take a deep inhale, followed by a slow exhale through your mouth. Feel your mind open up as you continue inhaling deeply through your nose and exhaling slowly through your mouth.

Again inhale deeply and exhale completely

If your mind starts to wander just let any errant thoughts pass through and release them like water flowing down a stream.

Let your breath center you. Let your breath calm you. Let your breath soothe you.

As you breathe in, feel healing energy come into your body like a warm soothing breeze that infuses every cell in your body.

As you exhale you are releasing any aches, pains and dysfunction from your body. With every inhale you are breathing in health and with every exhale you are releasing pain and discomfort.

Feel your body get lighter and lighter as you continue to release anything that is weighing you down.

Physical pain, stress, discomfort, fear. Let it all float away from you as you welcome the healing energy with every breath you take.

Find relief in release and embrace the healing energy that you are inhaling every time you breathe.

As you continue to breathe, feel your body growing stronger and any areas of weakness getting filled with vibrant healing energy.

You are activating deep healing in your life and you can feel your internal energy shift as you receive wonderful healing energy from the universe.

Allow yourself to feel that healing happening now. Feel it in every bit of your mind and your body.

Continue to sit in this healing energy giving yourself completely to it. You are open and free of any attachments to pain or discomfort. With every breath, you are freeing yourself from pain and welcoming healing.

Now take your right hand and place it on any part of your body where you feel any pain or discomfort. Feel your palm transfer calmness and healing energy to ease any pain and discomfort.

Repeat this affirmation quietly in your mind – I am free from pain and discomfort. I am healthy. I am full of healing energy.

As you affirm your health, continue breathing in deeply and exhaling slowly. Let your hand fall back to your side and trust that the healing energy you feel in your body is manifesting to free you from pain and discomfort.

Take another deep breath and feel the gratitude of being whole again. Picture yourself in perfect health and sit with this feeling as long as you need to.

Connect with the healthy you that you have visualized. Feel yourself in that body and let yourself claim it for yourself.

Now take a deep breath, hold it for a while then slowly exhale. As you breathe deeply, start to tune in to your breathing and slowly bring your awareness back to your body.

You can now slowly open your eyes and keep this feeling of healing and restoration with you throughout the day.

This guided meditation is now complete.

Freedom from Addiction Meditation - 20 minutes

Addictions are coping mechanisms that we use to distance ourselves from our pain. You may be addicted to alcohol, cigarettes, smoking or even drugs. However, no matter what the addiction is, the key is to find the emotional and psychological traumas that trigger the addictive tendencies. With meditation, you can start healing your addiction from the source instead of just dealing with the symptom.

This meditation will help you learn to cope with the emotional trauma that drives you to addictive behavior. If you want to manifest good health and wellbeing, it is important to align your emotional and mental health with the physical health you want to manifest.

Let's get into it.

Duration 20 minutes

Find a comfortable place to sit. You can do this meditation sitting up in a comfortable chair or lying down in a quiet room free of distractions.

Start by taking in a deep breath filling your lungs all the way hold, and then release through your mouth. As you exhale release any tension or anxiety you may have.

Let us do this another three times to completely calm yourself and open up your mind. Deep breath in, slow exhale. Deep breath in, slow exhale. Deep breath in, slow exhale.

Release all that tension, any anxiety and any errant thoughts in your mind. Deep slow breath in, again slowly exhale freeing yourself from anxiety and tension.

Now, return to your normal breathing pattern. Continue to inhale peace and relaxation and exhale anxiety, fear and self-doubt.

You are strong. You are in control of your emotions. You are in control of your habits. You are in control of your health.

Now breathing slowly, slowly ask yourself - what am I afraid of? What am I hiding from behind the cover of this addiction? Whether it is alcoholism or overeating or smoking or any other addiction name it clearly at this point whatever it is.

Let the answer rise unbidden to the surface. Do not try to judge or analyze the answer simply let it float to the surface of your consciousness.

Whatever the answer is acknowledge it and accept it. Whether you are running away from emotional pain, whether you are afraid of facing the unknown, whether you are trying to soothe past hurts. Whatever the reason is acknowledge it without judgment and sit with it for a minute.

Now take a deep breath and slowly exhale. Calm your mind by breathing in deeply and exhaling slowly through your mouth.

Now that you know what you are running from, ask yourself - what do I have to gain by holding on to this fear? What am I losing by hiding from my pain?

Again, just let the answer rise to the surface unbidden. Let your subconscious tells you what it already knows that you may not be aware of. Open yourself up to the answer and receive it without judgment.

Without judging allow whatever answers you have hidden and buried under the surface to rise to the surface.

As you receive the realization, continue with the deep breathing allowing the deep slow inhales to bring in positive healing energy. As you exhale release the pain, the hurt and the fear that you are feeling.

Let it all out. Feel the pain and release it even as you continue to breathe in healing energy.

Now ask yourself - what will I gain by letting go of this addiction? Again name your specific addiction clearly.

When the answer comes to you sit with it for a moment. Acknowledge it and open your mind to it.

Now take a deep breath, hold for a minute and then exhale slowly.

At this point start to visualize yourself sitting in a vast green garden surrounded by lush greenery.

You are sitting under a magnificent tree and you can feel a calm breeze caressing your skin. All around you, it is quiet and peaceful.

As you look up into the horizon, you can see that the sun is about to set. As you watch this beautiful sun start to set, bring your palms above your heart and repeat this affirmation out loud.

I release my pain. I release my addiction. I release my fear.

As you say these words feel your body get lighter and lighter with every exhale.

Repeat this affirmation out loud.

I welcome healing. I welcome health. I am free.

As you affirm your intentions, raise your arms and open them up as if you want to embrace the air all around you.

Repeat this affirmation out loud – I welcome healing. I welcome health. I am free.

Now let your arms fall back to your sides. Continue to look at the beautiful sunset. Breathe in the crisp clean air and let the soothing breeze caress your face.

The universe is giving you its healing power. You are getting the strength you need to move forward with confidence without hiding from your emotions.

You are free. You are well. You are at peace with yourself.

Allow yourself to experience this feeling of newness and refreshment. Lean into the healing power that is enveloping you right in this moment. Feel it and connect to it. Carry it with you.

When you are ready, slowly start to bring your awareness back to the present. Tune in to the rhythm of your breathing. Focus on the sensation of air entering and living your body.

Slowly open your eyes.

This guided meditation is now complete.

Guided Meditation for Anxiety and Sleep - 20 minutes

Good rest is not just essential for your mental well-being but also your physical health. Sleep is important for a healthy body, weight management and even dealing with stress. If you often toss and turn because of an overactive mind, a calming meditation will help you get the rest you need to stay mentally and physically healthy.

This guided meditation is intended to help you overcome anxiety and sleep peacefully. Do not practice this meditation while driving or operating any kind of equipment.

Let us get started.

Duration 10 minutes

Start by lying comfortably in your bed. Lie in the last position you remember falling asleep in or your usual sleeping position.

Now close your eyes and focus your attention on your body. Scan from the top of your head to your feet. As you bring your awareness to each part, release any tension and soften your muscles until you start to feel completely relaxed and at ease.

Now you are going to create in your mind a home base where we can go whenever you feel overwhelmed, anxious or scared.

This home base will become the place where you anchor your attention when your mind is overrun with anxiety, worry and other negative thoughts.

To create this home base, you will need to anchor it by becoming aware of your breathing.

Whenever you want to bring your mind to a calm peaceful place, you will focus all your awareness on your breathing. You will take deep breaths through the nose, then exhale slowly through the mouth.

As you inhale you breathe in a calming soothing energy, and as you exhale, you are releasing worry, stress and fear.

The more you continue to breathe in and out, the more calm energy you bring into your body and the more negative energy you expel.

This deep breathing will be your anchor to your home base where you go to quiet your mind.

As you breathe your attention is on the pace of your breathing, the sensations in your chest, the rise and fall of your abdomen and the sensations in your body. Any time you feel your mind wondering simply refocus your attention on the rhythm and sensations of your breathing.

Deep breath in, slow exhale.

You are anchoring your attention using your breath. Your body feels more and more relaxed and your mind is calm and free of any anxiety.

Now just allow your breathing to fall into a natural rhythm.

Start to visualize yourself on a long quiet beach. You are in the shade deeply relaxed and comfortable on a reclining chair that cushions your limbs perfectly.

You can see the blue and green ocean. The water is calm under a beautiful summer sky.

You can see the water shimmer as it touches the sandy shore in gentle waves that advance and retreat slowly.

There is a gentle breeze that is caressing your skin and you can feel a warm glow as you lie in your beach chair feeling connected to the peace and tranquility around you.

Notice the perpetual movement of the water against the shore and feel it start to lull you slowly into a comfortable daze.

You are drifting off slowly and all you can hear are the gentle sounds of the ocean and the breeze around you.

The gentle breeze is warm against your skin and there is complete peace and tranquility.

You are drifting deeper into relaxation as you feel the flow of the ocean bring you healing and serenity in this quiet and peaceful place.

Let yourself drift off in this quiet place. You are enjoying the tranquility and your mind is completely calm and relaxed.

Abandon yourself to the quiet and now let the gentle waves soothe you as you sleep.

Chapter 6: The Healing Room; Manifestations for Your Spirit

The law of attraction depends on our subconscious energy to manifest the things that we want to see in our lives. However, for most people, the law of attraction does not work because they lack clarity not just on what they want but also about who they are deep down inside. Meditation helps to open up the deepest layers of your subconscious to allow you to find the answers you need to manifest your desires.

To attract love, wealth, abundance and good health, it is important to have clarity. Clarity about who you are and where you want to go and clarity about the kind of energy you are projecting into the universe. If your internal energy is different from the things you want to manifest, you will always struggle to manifest the things you want. Your desires and your intentions need to be aligned with the subconscious energy that you are anchored to.

For this section, the meditations will focus on bringing your clarity, self-acceptance and mending any broken spirit that may be tainting your subconscious energy.

Meditation for Self-Love and Self-Acceptance - 20 minutes

Clarity starts with self-acceptance. Knowing who you are, what is important to you and where you want to go will help you align your internal energy with the things you truly want to manifest.

Let us get into it.

Duration 20 minutes

Start by making yourself comfortable in a quiet room. Sit in a comfortable chair with your feet firmly planted on the ground. Your neck and spine should be aligned in an upright but relaxed posture.

Now close your eyes gently. Place your hand on your chest above your heart then take a deep breath in through your nose. Exhale slowly and as you do release any pent-up thoughts or emotions.

Keep breathing in deeply, as you relax and exhale any tension or stress releasing it from your body.

You are feeling calmer and more relaxed as you continue to breathe in deeply and exhale slowly.

Allow each inhale to be a bit deeper than the one before it. Feel your lungs expand out as you inhale, and feeling everything contract back in as you exhale.

Now allow your breathing to return to its normal rhythm but continue to follow the sensations of your breath weaving in and out of your body.

Let your body and mind relax completely letting go of any tension, anxiety or errant thoughts.

Now turn your attention to the bottom half of your body, everything from your hips all the way down to the tips of your toes.

Bring your awareness to this part of your body and as you do feel a warm sensation traveling from your feet all the way up to your hips.

As you become more in tune with this part of your body now imagine that the awareness and warm sensation in this lower part of your body are radiating love and appreciation.

You are releasing positive energy to this part of your body. Embracing every curve, every scar and everything else about this part of your body. Feel the love and appreciation flow from your mind to your lower body.

Gradually continue to move your awareness upward and now focus on the top half of your body. Feel the warm sensation travel from your hips up into your abdomen, to the arch of your spine, up to your shoulders and to the very top of your head.

Now you can feel every part of your body vividly. You are sending love and appreciation to every inch of your body and allowing your awareness to ease any tense muscles.

As you appreciate and send love to your body repeat this affirmation quietly in your mind.

I am beautiful. Every part of me is perfect just as it is. I accept who I am. I appreciate who I am.

Now take a deep breath in and slowly release it through the mouth feeling your body relax even more.

Repeat this affirmation one more time.

I am beautiful. Every part of me is perfect just as it is. I accept who I am. I appreciate who I am.

And now begin to call to mind other parts of yourself that you've held in judgment in the past.

All the little things you nitpick about yourself and constantly berate yourself for. A bad decision, a missed opportunity, something you lost, something you failed at. Recall all the things that you hold against yourself for whatever reason.

Think of all the things you say about yourself that highlight your flaws and overlook your strengths. Let all these things come to the surface as one by one you sift through all the negative and self-defeating beliefs.

As you allow these thoughts to rise to the surface, begin to release them one by one. Every time you exhale, release these negative judgments that you have about yourself.

Release the self-doubt, the regrets, the guilt, the shame, the need for acceptance from others. Disconnect yourself from these judgments by letting them float away with every exhale.

Feel your mind and body start to get lighter as you unload all these judgments and negative beliefs that you have been carrying around with you.

Feel yourself getting freer and freer as you keep breathing out the negativity and cleansing your mind with fresh positive energy.

As you continue to release the negative thoughts repeat this affirmation quietly in your mind.

I offer myself forgiveness. I free myself from these negative thoughts and emotions. I offer myself acceptance. I am okay with who I am.

Now take in a deep breath and as you exhale open up your arms and reach out on either side.

With your arms wide open, visualize a bright golden light bathing you from the top of your head all the way to your feet.

As this light touches you, any negativity or tension in your body is being washed away and you feel a renewing energy engulf you.

Allow yourself to luxuriate in this light as you feel it take away any self-judgment leaving only love and acceptance.

Now bring your arms around yourself, hugging yourself and as you do so feel the love and appreciation you have for yourself.

At this point I want you to focus on the parts of you that you cherish and love the most. Whether it is your smile, your kind spirit, your love of nature, your strength, your resilience, a feature that you love.

Everything you appreciate and love about yourself, focus on it right now. Whatever makes you proud, whatever milestones you have reached so far, whatever challenges you have overcome.

Call to mind all the positive things about yourself and go through them one by one. Note each of them with appreciation and love. Let yourself connect with these positive thoughts and emotions that you have about yourself.

Now you can bring your arms back down. But stay in the moment a while longer simply focusing on everything you love about yourself and appreciating who you are.

When you are ready, you can bring your awareness back to the present by focusing on your breathing. Slowly become aware of your surroundings and gently open your eyes.

You can practice this meditation every time you find yourself having negative self-talk or when you simply want to lift your spirits and self-esteem.

This guided meditation is now complete.

Guided Meditation for Healing Broken Hearts & Removing Negative Attachments - 25 minutes

When you have been in a failed relationship or any kind of toxic relationship, often the emotional trauma stays with you long after the relationship ends. This trauma often leads to dysfunction in your subsequent relationships and makes it impossible for you to attract and manifest healthy and loving relationships. It is important to work on being whole by releasing negative attachments before you can seek to invite and attract new relationships.

This guided meditation will help you train your mind to release negative attachments that keep you anchored to toxic situations and environments.

Let us get started.

Duration: 25 minutes

Start by sitting or lying down in a comfortable position and allow yourself to relax your muscles.

Now close your eyes and take a few long deep breaths to help calm you and ease any tension.

Take a deep breath feeling the air enter your body and into your lungs. Feel your stomach and chest rise and fall as you inhale and exhale.

Feeling any tension and stress leave your body every time you exhale.

Notice the relief that it brings to your body and mind to release some of that tension and stress.

Now repeat the deep breathing a couple more times and sink even deeper into relaxation and calmness.

Now I want you to focus on any comfort that you feel no matter how small it is. Maybe it is the cozy temperature in your room, the comfortable chair you are sitting on or anything else that is bringing you some comfort in this moment.

As you hold on to this feeling of comfort start to visualize yourself sitting in front of a warm cozy fireplace. The fire is burning nice and warm and you can see the bright flames rising gently into the air.

As you sit in the warm glow of this fire, call to mind an experience, a memory or any past hurt that you would like to take and burn and be free of.

Let the image or memory come to you unbidden. Do not try to force it or rush it. Know that whatever image comes to mind first is the correct one.

Now take that image on the mental screen of your inner mind and let it be as big as a portrait. You can see it clearly in vivid detail as you hold it in your hand.

Now just toss it gently into the fire and watch it start to burn. See the flames starts to eat it up as it shrivels and starts to turn into ash. Watch it disappear completely into the flames until nothing is left but the warm glow of the fire.

Now I want you to take the next memory that brings you pain, hurt or regret. As you see this memory on the mental screen of your mind, see it as a portrait with that memory clearly painted on it.

Hold that portrait in your hand and then toss it into the flames and watch as it burns. Watch the smoke rise slowly into the air as the portrait catches fire. Watch it start to shrivel until it is completely engulfed in flames and there is nothing left.

Now repeat the same process for as many toxic memories, situations and people that you want to detach yourself from because they are keeping you from growing.

Clear all the residual hurts and attachments by burning them one by one in the fire until there is nothing left of them in you.

As you continue to release these attachments, feel your heart and mind get lighter and more open with each attachment that you release.

The bad relationships, the hurtful memories, any past hurts, you are releasing them all and unburdening yourself. You are freeing up space for the things that you want to manifest in your life.

You are releasing negative attachments to create room for new healthy relationships, new love, new happy memories and a life of abundance and joy.

Notice your level of peace or satisfaction as you untether yourself from all these unwanted attachments that have kept you from abundance and jot. Lean into this feeling of freedom, and peace.

Continue to gaze into the fire as it burns brightly bathing you in its cozy warmth. It is feeling you with a positive energy and you feel open and clear about who you are and where you want your life to go.

You have unshackled yourself and now there is room in your heart and your mind for new experiences, new memories and healthier relationships.

Allow yourself to sit with this realization for a moment. Revel in your release and detachment from all the things that were not serving you.

Now take a deep healing breath in and fill the crisp clean air fill your lungs before exhaling slowly.

Repeat the deep breathing two more times, then allow your breathing to go back to its normal rhythm.

Slowly start to bring your awareness to the present by focusing on your breathing. When you are ready you can gently open your eyes.

This guided meditation is now complete.

Guided Meditation for Forgiveness and Letting Go - 20 minutes

Nothing burdens your spirit and weighs down your mind like holding on to grudges, past hurts and judgments against yourself and others. If you want to radiate the positive energy that you need to manifest love, abundance and wealth, it is important to clear your conscience and unburden yourself.

The freedom that forgiveness brings allows you to direct your energy into the things you want rather than getting caught up in what you do not like. If all your energy is going towards grudges, hate for others, self-hate and other destructive emotions there is no way you can manifest a happy abundant life.

This meditation will allow you to forgive and let go freeing yourself to receive all the blessings the universe has in store for you.

Let us get into it.

Duration 20 minutes

Make yourself very comfortable in a seated position on the floor on a meditation cushion or in a chair. You can also choose to lie down with a pillow beneath your knees and another pillow supporting your neck and head.

Make sure you are as comfortable as possible. If any of your clothing is tight release it so that your body is not constrained in any way.

Your spine should be straight and your arms and legs uncrossed to ensure the natural flow of energy throughout your body

Now take several slow deep breaths feeling them all the way up through the top of your head and all the way down through to your legs.

Your breath is a life force so as you breathe in allow this life force to move deeply into your body bringing fresh life and energy into your body.

As you exhale allow this life force to wash away any physical and emotional toxins that you need to release.

Repeat this inhale and exhale cleansing a few times and with every inhale allow the life force to go deeper and with every exhale just let go of negativity and toxins.

Now allow yourself to be supported in this moment by calling on the universe to surround you with love and light. Allow the universe to surround you with its healing and protective energy and bring you healing.

Notice all the points of contact between your body and wherever you are resting and allow your body to melt more and more into relaxation with every breath.

You are safe. You are comfortable. You are in a good place.

Now start to picture pure white light beginning to fill up your room. This light is filling the entire room covering every inch of open space in your room.

Feel the white light wash over you in a gentle wave that brings nourishment and protective energy.

Now still enveloped in this light, picture a shimmering door before you. You know instinctively that this door is inviting you to a beautiful place beyond.

Notice the door in every detail. The color, the size, the shape, the texture. As you take in every little detail, now bring your attention to the doorknob.

Reach out and touch the doorknob feeling its coolness in your palm. Now take a deep breath, turn the knob and open the door.

On the other side of the door, you are standing on a serene white sandy beach overlooking an expansive crystal-clear blue ocean.

The sand beneath your feet feels warm and soft to your bare feet.

The warm rays of the sun feel warm and inviting. The air smells fresh and clean and every breath in feels like a cleansing energy working its way into your body.

Feel the gentle breeze caress your skin gently. It all feels so peaceful.

Now take a deep breath and inhale the fresh salty scent of the ocean as you listen to the soothing sounds of the waves.

Slowly walk to the water's edge and stand there feeling the gentle waves touch your feet as they advance and retreat from the shore.

You can feel the pure energy of a healing wave coming towards you. As you stand here at the edge, you open up your palms and as you do so, breathe in deeply and exhale slowly.

With every exhale you release from your mind and heart any grudges, any hate any past hurts that you are holding on to.

Continue to breathe in the cool healing life force of the pecan air and as you exhale, let all the things that you are holding against yourself and others go.

As you release these negative emotions repeat this affirmation quietly in your mind.

I forgive myself. I free myself from grudges and hate. I am opening myself up to love. I am radiating love. I am letting go.

As you affirm your intentions continue to breathe in the healing life force of the ocean and with every exhale continue to unburden yourself.

You are releasing from your heart anything you feel needs forgiving within yourself. Past actions, unhealthy habits, toxic behaviors, negative thoughts and all those negative beliefs that block your essence.

You are releasing any animosity you feel towards others and choosing to let go of grudges and unresolved issues because they are only clouding your clarity and preventing you from manifesting your desires.

You are releasing it all into the ocean and as you stand there you can feel all these negative thoughts and emotions get swept up in the waves.

With every release, you feel freer and more in control of your heart, your mind and your destiny.

You are no longer going to be driven by negative emotions. Instead, you will lean into your positive emotions and direct your energy to the things you want to attract in your life. Health, wealth, abundance and love.

At this point repeat this affirmation quietly in your mind.

I forgive myself. I free myself from grudges and hate. I am opening myself up to love. I am radiating love. I am letting go.

Now take a deep breath, hold it for a moment and exhale slowly. Another deep breath and as you inhale feel the healing life force touch every cell in your body.

Exhale slowly and let your breathing go back to normal.

Let this feeling of utter and complete unburdening and freedom wash over you. Feel the warm rays of the sun on your face and as you do, roll your shoulders back to open up your heart and your mind to the positive energy of the universe.

Gradually, bring your awareness back to the present. As you breathe, tune in to the sensations of the rhythmic rise and fall of your chest. Focus on these sensations until your awareness is back to the present.

You can now open your eyes.

This guided meditation is now complete.

Affirmations for Body, Mind and Soul - 10 minutes

Affirmations rewire your brain to create new core beliefs that create the reality that you want to manifest in your life. When you use affirmations to state and clarify your intentions you reset your beliefs to align with the things that you want to attract to your life and manifest.

You can repeat these affirmations every day in the morning or just before you go to bed.

Let's get started.

Duration: 10 minutes

Sit in a comfortable position. You can sit on a chair or on the floor wherever you feel most comfortable.

Straighten your spine and tuck your chin slightly inward to align your neck with your spine.

Now close your eyes and start to connect with your mind and body.

Tune in to your breathing and feel the air enter and leave your body. If any errant thoughts come to mind, simply release them and turn your focus back to your breathing.

As you feel your body and mind relax completely you can now repeat these affirmations. You can do it out loud or quietly in your mind.

I am a magnet for positivity and happiness.

I see the beauty of everything around me.

I am surrounded by love and I freely give my love to others.

I wake up every day excited to embrace the day.

I accept myself unconditionally.

I love and accept myself for who I am.

I am grateful for all the good things in my life.

I choose love over hate.

I choose forgiveness and freedom.

I am at peace with myself.

I am in tune with the universe and allow it to guide me.

I embrace joy and positivity every day.

Every day I get closer to my dreams.

My life is filled with possibilities and potential.

I focus on the positive and celebrate who I am.

I choose to be confident.

I choose to be at peace.

I choose to be free.

I am proud of who I am and the person I am becoming.

I am strong mentally physically and spiritually.

I live my life with grace and courage.

I am always surrounded by positive energy.

I am full of boundless positive energy

I trust the universe to guide me to my heart's desires.

I attract joy and positivity everywhere.

I focus on what I can control and let go of what I can't.

I have everything that I need to be happy and fulfilled

I give myself permission to be happy.

I embrace everything the universe is releasing to me right now.

Chapter 7: Overcoming Limiting Beliefs

When you think of the law of attraction, it is easy to assume that as long as you know what you want you can manifest it. However, since your subconscious is the reservoir of the energy you put out into the universe, you can only manifest the things you want if your beliefs are in alignment with what you want to manifest. You cannot manifest wealth if you are constantly thinking about lack. You cannot manifest love if you are convinced that you are unworthy of it. Your beliefs and your intentions must be aligned for the law of attraction to work.

Self-limiting beliefs will always be the biggest barrier to manifesting your desires. You must first believe in yourself and in what you want to achieve before you can call it into reality. Ultimately the universe will only give you what you have enough courage and belief to ask for.

To make it easier to reset your subconscious and rewire your mind, the meditations in this section are all about overcoming self-limiting beliefs that block your path to abundance.

Guided Meditation for Overcoming Self-Sabotage -25 minutes

If you find yourself constantly holding yourself back from going after the things you want either due to fear, lack of confidence or any other limiting beliefs, this meditation is for you. Self-sabotage is something that we do both consciously and subconsciously and it can make it difficult to live up to your full potential.

Let's get started.

Duration: 25 minutes

Start by sitting comfortably in a relaxed but upright posture. Relax your shoulders and make sure that your feet are firmly planted on the ground.

Now you are going to direct your awareness inward by shutting out all external input.

Take a nice big deep breath and as the air fills your lungs, feel yourself relaxing and releasing any tension. Exhale slowly through your mouth and feel the tension leave your body.

Now close your eyes and take a couple more deep breaths followed by slow exhales that lead you deeper into relaxation.

You can now allow your breathing to go back to normal.

I want you to now bring all your awareness to the bottoms of your feet. Imagine that there are cords connecting your feet to the ground, anchoring you and supporting you.

Now visualize a relaxing energy flowing up from the ground into your feet. You can feel your feet get warmer as this energy rises up into them filling them with a soothing warmness that starts to travel throughout your body.

You are feeling completely relaxed and every tension in your body has dissipated. Your muscles are loose and soft and all you feel is the comforting warmth of the energy coming from the ground and into your body.

Continue to focus on this pleasant and soothing feeling that is spreading throughout your body. You feel like a great weight has just been lifted from your shoulders.

It is so calm and peaceful and you feel yourself open up to receive the energy that is soothing and relaxing your entire body.

Now take a deep breath and as you do so think of a pattern of behavior or habit that you repeat even when you know it is not good for you.

I want you to see this pattern clearly and identify it in the way you live your life. Maybe it is procrastinating over important decisions. Maybe you always shy away from anything that challenges your perceived comfort zone. Maybe you always worry about failure.

Whatever it is that you repeatedly do, focus on this particular pattern and acknowledge it without judgment.

Now I want you to go back to the time to when the pattern began. Move as far back as you can in time until you uncover the source of the limiting belief.

Was it something you experienced as a child, something someone said that maybe made you question your self-worth? Is it a failure that you have trouble getting over?

Delve deep and allow yourself to find the trigger that created the pattern that you find yourself constantly repeating in your life.

You are right there now in the past. Take note of the details. Are you indoors or outdoors? Are you alone or is someone with you? What are you feeling in this moment?

As you immerse yourself in the memory notice the conditions that existed at this starting point of your pattern of self-sabotage. What is your mental state? How are you feeling emotionally? What is going on around you?

Now take time to think about how in similar circumstances you revert to this pattern because your subconscious is holding on to the negative experience or memory.

Take a moment to absorb any information in the scene from the past that will help you detach yourself from this negative pattern.

Are there any emotional ties that are causing you to keep repeating this pattern of behavior? Does it help you escape your fear or mask your emotions? Are you using this pattern to avoid challenging and pushing yourself?

Be open to receiving the answer without judgment or shame. Open yourself up to the realization that your self-sabotage is really just a reflection of your emotional resistance to things that you are not comfortable with.

As you start to become aware of the answers, see yourself moving back to the future from that time in the past that set off your destructive pattern.

As you withdraw from the memory, feel it fade further and further away from you until it is nothing but a tiny speck on the horizon.

You are releasing that memory right now and freeing yourself from its attachment in your life. You will not live your present based on your past and you are opening your mind up to new perspectives and new belief systems.

Keep withdrawing from that past memory and the further away you go, feel it sink deeper and deeper into oblivion. Picture yourself shutting a door and leaving that experience behind the closed door as you walk towards a different door.

You are standing before this new door and you can see it vividly in your mind. You can see the doorknob and you reach out and touch it. The cool metal feels soothing in your hand and you take a deep breath and open the door.

On the other side of the door, you are standing in a lush green field surrounded by a vast expanse of greenery and trees.

The air is clean and fresh and all around you are the nurturing sounds of nature.

A cool gentle breeze rustles the trees and you feel the crisp clean air fill your lungs as you breathe in.

You feel confident and relaxed in this peaceful place and your mind is fully receptive to the loving positive energy of the universe.

You immerse yourself in this feeling of confidence and positivity that is coursing through your body right now.

Your mind is free of mental blocks, you are sure of yourself and your intentions, you are at ease with where you are. You are trusting the universe to manifest your deepest desires for success, love and joy.

Now as you continue to stand in this lush field surrounded by positive uplifting energy start to see all the things that you want to manifest in your life.

See the career that you have always wanted but been too afraid to chase after. Think of the relationship you have always wanted but never dared to pursue.

Think of all the things and desires you have kept buried out of fear or self-doubt. See them clearly in your mind and as you continue to visualize them open up your hands with your palms facing upwards ready to receive.

Feel the universe start to release all these things to you one by one. It is giving you all the things you have ever desired and all you have to do is reach out and take them.

Now bask in the confidence of knowing what you want is still out there waiting for you. Relax in the knowledge that what you are seeking is also seeking you if only you will allow yourself to find it.

Feel yourself yield to the infinite power and positive energy of the universe.

Remain in this space for a moment, attaching yourself to the positive energy and letting it fill you completely from the soles of your feet to the top of your head.

You are in sync with your desires, you know what you want and you are no longer afraid to reach out and take it.

Now slowly start to bring your awareness back to the present. Take a deep healing breath, hold for a moment then exhale slowly. Another slow deep breath followed by a long exhale.

Start to bring awareness back to your body. feel your arms, your feet and your chest as it rises rhythmically every time you breathe in and out.

When you are ready, open your eyes.

This guided meditation is now complete.

Reprograming Limiting Beliefs & Finding Your Power -15 minutes

Limiting beliefs can keep you feeling small and prevent you from living up to your potential. This meditation is intended to help you reprogram the negative thoughts and beliefs you have about yourself that are blocking you from manifesting abundance, success and wealth.

Let's get into it.

Duration: 15 minutes

You can choose to lie down or sit down in a comfortable position. Sit in a quiet room free of distractions and noise.

Now gently close your eyes and as you do so start to center and calm your mind by breathing deeply and bring all your awareness to the rhythm of your inhales and exhales.

Feel the sensations in your chest and abdomen as you inhale deeply letting the air fill your lungs. As you exhale slowly feel your chest relax.

As your body and mind start to relax, sink deeper into your chair or bed, allowing your muscles to soften and relax completely. Allow your body to sink deeper and deeper into relaxation with every breath you take.

Now that your awareness is fully focused inward, allow your breathing to return to its normal rhythm. Feel yourself fall deeper into yourself and sinking to a safe space within where there is no judgment or fear.

Now picture yourself walking barefoot on a soft thick bed of grass that is softly caressing your feet as you walk. Feel the coolness of the grass under your feet and fully allow it to support and anchor you.

You feel safe and at peace.

Your mind feels wide open and you are ready to open yourself up to new truths and release any beliefs that no longer serve you.

Take a deep breath and prepare yourself to absorb new truths into your subconscious.

Now repeat these affirmations.

I am worthy

I am lovable.

I exist. I matter. I am meant to be here.

I have a purpose.

I am confident and sure of myself.

I am surrounded by love and I attract it effortlessly to myself.

I am surrounded by wealth and I attract it effortlessly to myself.

I am beautiful inside and out.

I trust myself and my decisions.

I trust in my abilities and my potential.

I attract abundance like a magnet.

I embrace and accept who I am.

I trust the universe to manifest all my desires.

I exist. I matter. I am meant to be here.

Take a deep breath in and as you exhale, allow all of these new truths to sink in deeper into your unconscious mind.

Now repeat these affirmations.

I now cut all cords from negative beliefs in my life.

I detach myself from self-doubt, fear of failure and negativity.

I release all the dysfunctional circumstances and people in my life.

I am releasing negativity and making room for positivity and love.

I cleanse myself of all misconceptions and judgments about myself.

I free myself from the judgments of others.

As you affirm your new beliefs, feel the energy surging from the green grass beneath your feet into your body. It is a healing energy. It is a restoring energy. It is infusing you with love and self-acceptance.

Allow yourself to feel this positive energy permeate every cell of your being. As you breathe in, let the positivity flood your mind and your emotions and cleanse you of any dark limiting thoughts.

Now take a deep breath and repeat these affirmations.

I exist. I matter. I am meant to be here.

I have a purpose.

I am confident and sure of myself.

As you complete these affirmations, go into deep breathing to slowly start bringing your awareness to the present.

Deep breath in, hold for a moment, now exhale slowly through your mouth. Again slowly deep breath in through your nose, followed by a long exhale. Now allow your breathing to go back to normal.

Slowly open your eyes when you are ready.

This guided meditation is now complete.

Meditation for Eliminating Your Abundance and Success Blocks - 15 minutes

It is natural to see opposition and resistance when it is coming from external sources. However, we often overlook the ways in which our belief systems and subconscious energy block our own paths to success.

If you want to eliminate the self-imposed blockages that are keeping you from manifesting abundance in your life. Practice this guided meditation. It is intended to help you get out of your own way and reframe your mind to reflect all the things that you want to be manifested in your life.

Let us get started.

Duration 15 minutes

Find a comfortable quiet spot and sit in a comfortable posture. Relax your neck and shoulders and plant your feet firmly on the ground.

Now, I want you to look up as if you're looking into your eyebrows. Try and focus on the midpoint on your forehead which is a powerful chakra point that helps to open up your subconscious.

Now close your eyes with your awareness still focused on this chakra point.

Breathe in deeply and breathe out. Again, breathe in deeply and exhale slowly. You are starting to feel relaxed and calm.

Take another deep breath followed by a slow exhale and as you exhale release any tension that you are holding in your body. Let your muscles soften and allow your body to sink deeper and deeper into relaxation.

Now allow your breathing to go back to normal.

Slowly stretch your arms out in front of you as if you're holding onto the handlebars of a bike

Now with your arms still extended, visualize that you have a bucket in your left hand. This bucket is a vivid red and it is full of sand. The bucket is heavy and you can feel it weighing your extended arm down.

Your left arm is becoming heavier and heavier as you continue to hold the heavy bucket of sane. You can feel the tension start to grow in your left arm muscles.

On the other arm, your right hand is still extended. However, in this arm, all you have is a balloon. This beautiful balloon is not heavy at all so there is no strain on your right arm.

The beautiful balloon is pulling your arm up and you can feel your right up floating weightless before you.

As the weight of the sand bucket in your left hand continues to weigh you down, the helium balloon is trying to pull you up into the sky with it.

You are now being pulled in two different directions and you have a choice to let go of one of the things you are holding on to.

In your left hand is the red bucket full of sand. This bucket is a reflection of all your negative beliefs that keep you anchored in lack, unhappiness and emotional turmoil.

This red bucket contains your beliefs that there is not enough money, your belief that no one will love you as you are, your belief that you can only be rich if you came from wealth. This bucket is holding all your limiting beliefs and the longer you continue to hold it the more the strain on your left hand is.

You can feel the muscles in your left arm start to tire. This fatigue is slowly creeping into other parts of your body.

Now, look at the beautiful balloon on your right arm. This balloon is doing its best to help you float but the bucket in your other hand is too heavy to lift.

In this moment I want you to feel the weight of the red bucket on your left arm and feel the lightness in your right hand.

At this point, you have a choice. You can let go of the balloon and continue to struggle with the heavy bucket or you can let go of the bucket and allow the balloon to pull you up.

In this moment, you are realizing that you cannot hold on to both. The beautiful balloon is the abundance and success you want to achieve. It is all the things you want to manifest in your life.

However, to hold on to this balloon and let it pull you as high as you can go you must first release the bucket in your left hand.

Now take a deep breath and exhale slowly. Now tell yourself- I'm ready to let go of my fear. I'm ready to rise to my full potential. I'm ready to release these beliefs that have held me down for so long.

Now slowly open the palm of your left hand and let the bucket of sand fall to the ground. Your arm is no longer weighed down by the weight and you can feel the tension in your muscle start to ease.

Your whole body starts to feel lighter and lighter and slowly the beautiful balloon starts to pull you up into the sky. You are floating off the surface now, and the higher you rise the easier it becomes.

You are elated by this feeling of freedom and discovery that is engulfing you right now. You are ready to reach new heights and you have completely detached yourself from all the beliefs that were holding you sown.

Feel yourself rise steadily into the air as positive energy starts to fill your body with confidence and trust that you are on your way to meet your heart's desires.

Your wealth is weighting for you, your abundance is just a breath away and fulfilling relationships are in your sights.

See yourself steadily floating away from negative beliefs and rising higher and higher. It feels great to be free. You are allowing yourself to trust the universe to guide you to your dreams.

You have given up all resistance, all negative anchors and are opening yourself up to receive from the universe.

Let this feeling permeate every part of your being and sit with it for a moment. See the doors that are opening up for you right now after unburdening yourself. See the boundless possibilities that await you.

Now take a deep breath in, hold it in and then exhale slowly. Again, breathe deeply, and exhale. Now slowly let your consciousness return to the present. Become aware of your body, your surroundings and your breathing.

When you are ready, you can open your eyes.

This guided meditation is now complete.

Feeding Your Passions Using Meditation - 15 minutes

Do you often find yourself losing your motivation to pursue the things you want? Have you ever started to do something and then given up halfway through? If you keep birthing dreams that never come to pass because you cannot summon the energy to keep them going, mindful meditation can help you to keep feeding your passions.

In this meditation, you will learn how to reconnect to the things that are meaningful to you in order to manifest your desires.

Let's get into it.

Duration 15 minutes

Start in a comfortable position. You may sit cross-legged or with your knees together back on your heels. If you are sitting on the floor, get some cushy pillows to make yourself as comfortable as possible.

Now sit up nice with your spine is elongated and in alignment with your neck for an upright but relaxed posture.

Roll your shoulders back without straining to open up your chest and leave yourself open to receiving energy from the universe.

Now take a deep breath in and as you inhale roll your shoulders up towards your ears.

Exhale slowly through your mouth and roll your shoulders down. Start to ground yourself by bringing awareness to the surface beneath you. Become aware of all the parts of your body that are in contact with the surface you are sited on.

Take a moment to get grounded here and really root yourself down by visualizing cords connecting to the ground beneath and keeping you grounded and supported.

Now that you are truly centered I want you to ask yourself – what do you really want? What are you passionate about? If you could have everything you wanted right now what would you pick?

Listen to the answer that comes unbidden to the surface. Do not try to analyze or judge the answers just acknowledge what your subconscious is telling you.

Whatever the answer is feel it take hold in your mind and see it in vivid detail.

Maybe you want to start a business, maybe you want to pursue a different career, maybe you want to start a family, maybe you want to buy your first home. Whatever the answer is, recognize it and internalize it.

Feel yourself connect to whatever goals and passions you have uncovered for yourself. Imagine yourself having those things right now in this moment and how it would make you feel. Allow yourself to experience this feeling deeply and stay connected to it.

Now take a deep breath in, and then exhale slowly. Two more deep breaths in, followed by a slow exhale.

Now focus all your attention on your heart space by imagining a radiant bright light burning in your chest area. Feel the energy start to spread out from your heart into your arms, your eyes, your legs, your feet and every single cell in your body.

Feel yourself start to vibrate with this powerful energy that is filling you on the inside and radiating outside.

With this energy still coursing through your body, I want you to picture the passion or goal that you uncovered earlier. As you visualize this goal open up your mind and let this energy breathe life into this goal.

Now it is not just a house that you want, but you can see yourself living in it in your mind right now. It is not just a new job you want but you can picture yourself walking into your new office and sitting behind the desk.

Whatever your goal is breathe life into it by attaching yourself to it as the powerful radiant energy continues to radiate from you.

Don't just see yourself achieving it but also put yourself in that moment and feel what it will feel like to see your goal come to life.

Take a deep breath in and slowly exhale. Another deep breath in and a slow exhale. Now repeat this affirmation out loud.

I am committed to my goal. I have what it takes to achieve my purpose. I am attracting all the things I desire to my life.

As you voice your affirmation, bring your hand up to your chest and repeat these affirmations.

I can do anything I put my mind to.

I will pursue my goals to the very end.

I have what it takes to manifest my goals.

I am capable. I am strong. I am confident.

Sit with the power of your intentions and let these affirmations sink deep into your subconscious. Allow yourself to connect with them deeply and carry them with you.

Now slowly start to bring your awareness back to the present. Listen to the sound of your breath, feel the rhythm of your chest moving up and down and reconnect with the present.

When you are ready open your eyes.

This guided meditation is now complete.

Affirmations to Achieve Your Goals - 10 minutes

When you speak affirmations you are not just voicing the things that you want to manifest but you are also setting a clear intention that will guide you in the right direction. The following affirmations are powerful statements that will help you reset your mind when you start to lose motivation and commitment to your goals.

Repeat these affirmations in the morning for at least 21 days to reawaken your commitment to your goals.

Duration 10 minutes

Take a sit in a comfortable position and close your eyes.

To clear your mind and tap into your subconscious take a couple of deep breaths making sure to release any tension in your body as you exhale.

Again, breathe deeply and focus all your awareness on the air as it enters your body and fills your lungs. Exhale slowly through your mouth releasing any tension, errant thoughts and pent-up emotion.

One more time, deep inhale, hold for a minute then exhale slowly. As you feel your mind start to relax and calm down, allow your breathing to return to normal and repeat these affirmations.

Every day I take action to achieve my goals.

My mind is focused on getting things done.

Achieving success comes easily to me.

Nothing that can stop me from achieving success.

Being focused and motivated comes easily to me.

I act with courage and confidence.

I will take action to get things done.

My mind is energized, clear and focused on my goals.

All of my goals are well within my reach.

I am focused and consistent.

Everything I am seeking is also seeking me.

I have intense passion and belief in my goals.

I am aligned with the abundance of the universe.

I have everything I need to reach my goals.

The universe brings me success every day.

Chapter 8: Manifesting Personal Growth Through Healing

Progress is proof of life and every day we strive to be better than who we were yesterday. If you have been struggling to attract the things that you want, you can use meditation to boost your personal growth by rewiring your mindset. When you move from strength to strength and milestone to milestone, it is only a matter of time before you can manifest the wealth, abundance and love that you desire.

Just like everything else in life, manifesting your desires is an inside job that starts with having your mind and subconscious energy in the right place.

Guided Meditation for Self-Assertion-Discovering your Ideal Self - 25 minutes

It is so easy to lose yourself in the hustle and bustle of life. This guided meditation is designed to help you reconnect with your ideal self. You will start manifesting growth by rediscovering your worth and your higher purpose.

Let us get started.

Duration: 25 minutes

Start by finding a quiet space that is free of distractions and noise.

Now sit in a comfortable chair or on a meditation pillow on the floor. Relax your body and allow yourself to ease any tension in your muscles.

Now close your eyes and begin to bring your awareness to your breath without changing your normal breathing rhythm. Simply tune in to the gentle rise and fall of your chest as you breathe in and out.

Notice how your breath flows in through your nose and fills up your body with life. Notice how each exhale flows out taking with it emotional and physical stress.

Feel the stress and tension gradually melt away as you continue to focus your awareness on your breathing.

If you still have thoughts going through your mind simply let them flow through your mind without attaching to them.

Any time an errant thought pops into your mind simply draw your focus away from it by focusing on your breathing.

Gradually start to take deeper and longer breaths as you ease your mind and body deeper and deeper into relaxation.

Notice the stillness that comes between each inhale and exhale.

As your breath deepens focus your attention on the stillness between the breaths.

Take another deep slow breath in and fill your lungs completely and then release the breath through your mouth slowly and gently like a sigh.

Empty your lungs completely and feel all the tension in your body ease then allow your breathing to return to its natural rhythm.

Each breath is carrying you deeper and deeper into a calm, centered and relaxed state.

Your mind is open to possibilities and you feel a sense of clarity that is connecting you deeply with your subconscious.

Now allow yourself to let go of expectations, of the need to control and any resistance. Simply open your heart and your mind to what the universe has to offer. You are receptive and open.

Now bring your attention to the top of your head and imagine there is a warm light surrounding you and protecting you.

Visualize this light as a bright yellow light that is glowing softly and calming you as it passes over your body and bathes you in its radiance.

Every part of your body that this light touches feels lighter and softer.

Notice the glowing nature of the radiant light and lean into the relaxing and comforting energy that it is infusing you with.

You can feel your forehead soften. The muscles around your eyes are relaxed and your neck and shoulders are perfectly at ease. As the light travels down your body, you feel the relaxing warmth spread downwards and cover every inch of your body.

Each part of your body is connected to this radiant energy and you can feel the energy grounding you and supporting you.

With each breath begin to feel that you are fully supported by the surface beneath you and protected by the energy surrounding you.

Notice how calm and at peace you feel right now in this moment.

Now I want you to visualize yourself outside on a wooded trail. As you walk on this trail take in your surroundings in vivid detail. The feel of the breeze on your skin, the rays of sunshine peering down the tree branches, the slope of the ground beneath your feet and the path outlined ahead of you as you walk.

You can feel the gentle warmth of the sun on your skin and the clean crisp air feels divine every time you inhale.

As you walk along the trail, you can see a small lake up ahead. It is full of striking blue water that is calm and gently rippling with the breeze.

You are walking towards the lake and when you get to the bank you are now looking out at the sparkling blue with its reflections of the sky and the trees.

As you stand by this beautiful lake start to explore your innermost desires and values.

What do you want to manifest in your life? Who is the person you wanted to grow up to be when you are young?

What is the last thing you think about when you go to bed? What is the first thing you think about when you wake up in the morning?

As you begin this self-inquiry the answers will start to surface from your subconscious into your conscious thoughts.

Take time to explore what your subconscious is telling you. Now as you start receiving your answers reflect on whether the way you live is in alignment with the values you are uncovering.

When was the last time you did something that truly made you happy? How often do you take time to simply take care of yourself and appreciate yourself? Are you pursuing any of the dreams that are close to your heart?

As you continue with self-inquiry your gaze is still on the beautiful lake scenery before you. You are accepting the answers to your question without shame or judgment.

Now start to reflect on how you live your life and ask yourself how much of your life is dedicated to pleasing others as opposed to doing what is meaningful to you. How often do you compromise your values just to fit in or go along with everyone else?

Let every answer reveal to you where you are going and whether you are making progress towards your goals, standing still or walking backward.

Accept these revelations without fear and judgment knowing that with this awareness you can make different choices and steer your life in a direction that reflects your innermost values and desires.

As you continue to gaze at the lake, connect with your innermost desires that your self-inquiry has revealed to you.

Attach to those things that have been lying dormant under the surface waiting for you to pick them up, dust them off and give them the attention you deserve. These are your dreams, your values and the things that matter to you most.

Pick them up one by one, holding them tightly in your hand and committing to staying true to them.

Now take a deep breath and repeat these affirmations.

I choose to live with passion.

I choose to be true to my innermost desires.

I choose to live with my whole heart.

I choose to live life on my own terms.

I choose abundance in all aspects of my life.

I choose an authentic life.

I choose growth and progress.

I choose me.

Now that you have affirmed your commitment to living in alignment with your personal values, slowly allow yourself to feel deeply connected to your innermost desires and passions. Open your mind to being true to these desires and making them come true.

Now gradually start to bring your awareness back to the present moment. Start to feel your breath flowing in and out of your body. bring your focus to your legs, your arms, your neck and your spine.

You are feeling relaxed yet energized. You have clarity in your intentions and you feel centered and at peace.

When you are ready, gently open your eyes.

This guided meditation is now complete.

Finding Growth Through Struggle Guided Meditation - 20 minutes

Even with our best-laid plans, sometimes life simply does not go our way. While failure is a natural process of any growth curve, often constant disappointment and struggle can sour your spirit and diminish your hope for abundance, success, and joy.

This next meditation is designed to help you find the sun even in your darkest times and stay anchored in your dreams and goals trusting the universe to manifest them.

Let's get into it.

Duration 20 minutes

Find a comfortable place to practice this meditation. You can choose to sit on a comfortable chair or lie down.

Now close your eyes and start to calm your body and mind by taking a slow deep breath followed by a slow exhale through the mouth.

As you exhale, release any tension in your muscles and any pent-up emotions.

Simply concentrate on your breathing and releasing any stress that you are feeling right now.

Continue to breathe deeply sending the air all the way to the bottom of your diaphragm. Hold the breath for a moment then exhale slowly through your mouth.

With every deep breath, your body is relaxing, your muscles are softening and your mind feels centered and calm.

Every exhale is bringing your release from negative thoughts, anxiety and stress.

You feel more relaxed and peaceful now.

Your entire body is at ease and there is a calming soothing energy settling all around you.

Now allow your breathing to go back to its normal rhythm. In this relaxed state, I want you to call to mind the challenge or challenges that have drained you and left you feeling empty or broken.

Maybe it is a broken marriage, a relationship that did not go the way you wanted, losing the job of your dreams, illness, loss or anything else that has drained you of hope and faith.

Sit quietly with these thoughts and allow this memory to rise to the surface. It may be painful and you can probably still feel the hurt right now. But the only way to detach yourself from it is to acknowledge it, feel it and release it.

Sit with this experience and notice how it makes you feel thinking about it. Now take a deep breath and with this experience still in your mind, bring your hand up to your chest and inhale deeply, as you exhale. Now feel yourself releasing this experience with the breath that you are letting out.

See it float away from you and disappear into thin air. Take another deep breath, hold it for a few seconds.

Again as you exhale, release the memory of the struggle that you went through or are going through. Feel it leave your body and see it float away from you and disappear into thin air.

Now the next time you inhale, I want you to feel the fresh life force in the air come into your body and start to replace all the negative emotions that the experience triggered in you.

Feel the disappointment and the hurt get replaced by hope. Feel the need to control the outcome get replaced by surrender to the universe. Feel yourself replace stress with hope and joy.

The dark energy is leaving your body and renewing energy is replacing it. As you continue to inhale and exhale you are trading positivity for negativity, joy for sadness, despair for hope and control for surrender.

In this moment you are aware that even when you cannot control every external circumstance, you can always control how you let them affect you. You are reclaiming power over your emotions, your mindset and your reactions.

With every deep breath, you feel new life being breathed into every organ of your body. With every exhale you are unburdening yourself of disappointments, frustrations and fear.

You realize that you do not need to always control everything because the universe knows what you need.

Your desires are manifesting now as you change negative energy into powerful positive energy.

With your hands still over your heart repeat these affirmations.

I am attracting new opportunities and positivity.

I am freeing myself from the struggles of my past.

I deserve to succeed.

I am manifesting my deepest desires.

I trust the universe to give me exactly what I need.

I deserve happiness.

I deserve joy.

I am hopeful and confident about my future.

I can handle any challenge that comes my way.

I yield to the positive energy and open myself to it completely.

I will trust my journey and enjoy the process.

I am taking the first step towards a positive new life now.

Every day I will wake with hope and confidence.

Every day I will align my intentions with the energy of the universe.

I am attracting joy.

I am attracting abundance and wealth.

I am attracting good healthy and emotional healing.

I am whole.

As you affirm your intentions feel these words connect deeply with your subconscious. Do not just say them, feel them and understand what they mean. For every affirmation feel it happen as you say it. Allow it to manifest in your mind so that it can manifest in reality.

Now take a moment to repeat the affirmations that particularly resonate with you. Make your own declaration right now and attach yourself mentally, emotionally and spiritually to it.

Take a deep breath in and allow yourself time for these uplifting affirmations to sink in. Let yourself attach to them deeply and commit them to your heart and mind.

When you are ready, start to bring your awareness back to your body and your surroundings. Take a deep breath in and then exhale slowly. Again, inhale deeply and then exhale slowly through your mouth.

Embrace the feeling of optimism and positivity that you are feeling right now in this moment. You can now gently open your eyes.

This guided mediation is now complete.

Emotional Healing and Liberating Yourself From Toxic Relationships - 25 minutes

If you have been wounded by a partner or a loved one in a way that left you emotionally damaged you can still manifest healthy and fulfilling relationships. This mediation is best practiced in bed just before you sleep to help you nurture your emotional health and manifest the kind of love you deserve.

Let's get started.

Duration 25 minutes

Start by lying in bed. Lie in your normal sleep position ensuring that you are comfortable and that there are no distractions in your room.

Now gently close your eyes and listen to the sound of my voice as I take you deeper into relaxation.

If you hear any sounds, let them calm your mind and soothe you.

If you have any tension in your body, bring your awareness to that part of your body and as you breathe out release that tension and feel your muscles soften and relax.

Concentrate on your breathing, each breath relaxing you more and more until you feel your body sinking and melting into the bed.

Now, visualize yourself in a garden. The air is clean and fresh and all around you is the beauty of nature and its tranquility.

It's as if the world has not touched this magical garden. The colors are vibrant and rich. Just ahead of you there are beautiful flowers of different shades and as you get closer to them you can smell a sweet inviting fragrance that is drawing you in.

Take a deep breath in and inhale the warm and perfumed air and as you breathe out, relax deeper and deeper.

As you continue walking in this magnificent garden, you can feel the cool grass under your feet.

As you breathe in the fresh air of the garden you can feel your body getting more refreshed with each breath you take.

You feel safe and relaxed.

As you continue walking you come to a pathway lined with stones that lead to a beautiful beach.

There are 10 stones on this pathway and each has unique healing properties.

As you step on that first stone, you feel yourself becoming more relaxed and at ease with yourself.

You come to the 9th stone and as you step on that stone, you're surrounded by a protective bubble that makes you feel safe and protected.

Take the next step to stone number 8 and feel a deep sense of peace settle within you.

Seven, you feel a sense of confidence. This is the stone that invokes the brain and awakens your subconscious.

Six, you are feeling calm and relaxed.

Five, your subconscious is fully listening to everything I say

Four, you feel yourself letting go of any tension and stress in your body.

Three, the mind, body and spirit are all aligned and in tune with the healing energy of the universe.

Two, breathe deeply and sink into the warm embrace and positive energy the universe is giving you.

One, sleep, deeper down as you reach the beautiful beach.

You are now at the beach and as you gaze into the distance, you see the vastness of the sea.

You are watching the waves roll gently towards the beach then retreat once they reach the shore.

As you walk to the water's edge, you can see your reflection in the water. Your face looks calm, happy and content.

Your feet sinking into the warm sand and you know without a doubt that you are exactly where you're supposed to be

As you drift deeper into this world you strip away the negative things that surround you.

You release the toxic attachments in your life that are stealing your joy.

You release yourself from relationships that only cause you pain.

You accept yourself as you are with all your strengths and flaws.

You can see all the positives that surround you in your life.

You now realize that the hurt and the pain of the past are only a minor part of who you are.

You start to have gratitude for who you are and who you'd become.

You forgive yourself. For your past. For your choices. For settling for less than you deserve. For forgetting that you are an amazing person.

Now you are stripping away any guilt that keeps you tethered to a toxic situation. You are freeing yourself from shame, from responsibility for other people's choices and constant pain.

You deserve better. You can do better. You will do better.

Let go of the past because the past doesn't serve you anymore.

Now, I want you to just take a moment and let your mind drift. Enjoy how relaxed your body feels.

I just want you to think of the word 'love'. Let it permeate your mind, body and spirit. Connect with it for a moment.

What does this word mean to you? How do you want to be loved? How do you want to love? What would your ideal relationship look like?

The answers to these questions are what you are going to manifest from this point onward in your life. Here them clearly and internalize them in your mind.

Today is the day you create the love you want and start to live a life you love. Today, you choose, and there is so much power in that choice.

Today is the day you love and respect yourself. You feel self-worth welling up inside of you, flowing through your body inspiring and healing you

Feel that energy flow through your heart and heal your spirit. It's time for your heart to heal.

It's time to leave the past in the past. It's okay to let go

Now, you can allow yourself to drift off safe and secure in the positive energy surrounding you.

This guided sleep meditation is now complete

Affirmations for Manifesting Growth - 5 minutes

Thoughts have the power to shape your reality and that is why affirmations are one of the core ways that you can use the law of attraction to manifest your goals and desires.

These powerful affirmations will help you align your mindset and your intentions to manifest the things you need in your life.

Duration: 5 minutes

Start by clearing your mind and making yourself comfortable.

Take a deep breath in and hold it for a while before exhaling. As you exhale feel any tension and stress in your body start to dissipate.

Take another deep breath in through the nose, hold for a moment and exhale slowly. Ome more deep breath in, hold and then exhale slowly through your mouth.

You feel calm and your mind is receptive. In this relaxed state, repeat the following affirmations.

I accept that my well-being and happiness are my responsibility.

I am embracing this day with gratitude.

I am opening up my mind and heart in gratitude for the good things that are on their way to me now.

I am aligning with my values, my intentions and my goals.

I will pursue my dreams with courage and passion.

I allow my light to shine brightly from today.

I am awakening to the greatness within me.

I am grateful for the healing energy of the universe.

I am grateful for the freedom I have to be myself.

I am grateful for everything in my life right now.

I gratefully and graciously accept all the things that I manifest in my life.

I am grateful for the lessons life has taught me.

I choose to learn from my challenges and move courageously forward.

I choose to move into abundance.

I choose to appreciate myself just as I am.

I choose to love myself fully.

I choose to show up in my life and live with hope and love.

Now you can open your eyes and breath in deeply allowing these affirmations to connect deeply with your subconscious.

You can repeat these affirmations every day in the morning to stay grounded and committed to your personal growth.

Chapter 9: Meditations for Your Mind

One of the reasons why meditation is such a powerful manifestation tool is because it is one of the most effective ways to reset your mind. When you want to get past destructive habits, negative emotions, limiting beliefs and any other success blockers, mediation provides the tool that you can use to tap into your subconscious.

Every outcome that you are living right now is a direct result of your mindset and your subconscious energy. This means to manifest success, abundance, wealth and even good health you must first create all these things in your mind then release them into the universe to become reality.

The meditations in this section are going to help you tap into the infinite power of the mind to manifest and attract success, abundance and wealth.

Meditation for Productivity and Focus - 10 minutes

If you struggle with productivity and getting things done, this guided meditation is a great way to start your day.

Let us get started.

Duration: 10 minutes

Start by making yourself comfortable. Sit in a comfortable chair with your feet planted on the ground.

Now relax your shoulders and sit upright with your neck and spine aligned. Now gently close your eyes.

Bring your awareness and focus to your breathing and let everything else fade into the background. Release any thoughts and simply tune into the rhythmic rise and fall of your chest as you breathe in and out.

As you inhale, feel the breath enter and nourish your body. As you exhale feel any stress and tension leave your body.

Continue to focus on your breathing and allow yourself to get into a relaxed state with every breath you take.

Now I want you to sit quietly and call to mind all the things you want to achieve today. See them clearly one by one and connect these things with your short-term and long-term goals.

As you continue to see these tasks, I want you to visualize yourself doing them. If it is an office or school project, visualize yourself working on it and finishing it. If it is a decision you need to make, visualize yourself having made it.

Whatever it is that you know that you need to do today, see yourself doing it and doing it well. Once you visualize this, allow yourself to feel the sense of accomplishment you will feel once you have completed it.

You are proud of yourself for having taken a step towards your goals and you know that each task you complete brings you closer to manifesting the things you want.

Now allow yourself to focus on your upper chest, really feel it puffing out as you breathe in and contract as you breathe out

Let the energy circulate up into your chest and wake up your mind and body. You are feeling invigorated, focused and energized.

Allow yourself to feel the rejuvenation of fresh breath, a fresh new perspective and a new day.

Your mind and body are eager to experience this new day and you embrace the things that you will do today.

Your mind is alert, your body is energized and you are radiating positive energy and manifesting productivity and success for your day.

Today you are in alignment with your intentions, your goals and your deepest desires.

You cannot wait to start taking steps to the things you want by doing everything you need to do and do it well.

You are grateful for the opportunity to manifest success, abundance and wealth.

This is your day and you will walk into it with confidence and purpose.

Now I want you to visualize yourself at the end of the day. You are feeling content and happy because you accomplished everything you wanted to do today.

Tune into this feeling of accomplishment. Connect with it and know that this is exactly how you want to feel at the end of the day.

Now take a deep slow breath in through your mouth. As you do this bring your awareness to the present. As you exhale slowly feel any trepidation about your day dissipate.

You are breathing in confidence and exhaling self-doubt. With every breath in you are surer of your purpose and your goals. With every breath out you feel any self-doubt and resistance disappear.

Now allow your breathing to go back to normal. When you are ready you can open your eyes.

This guided meditation is now complete.

Guided Meditation for Overcoming Procrastination - 20 minutes

One of the biggest blocks people face to manifesting wealth and abundance is procrastination and putting off action. To attract the things that you desire, you must be willing to act and set in motion the opportunities that will create the outcomes you want.

This guided meditation is meant to help you become more decisive and proactive.

Let's get into it.

Duration: 20 minutes

Make sure that you are in a comfortable position. You can choose to sit on a chair or a meditation pillow on the floor.

Place your arms gently on your lap and close your eyes to begin focusing your awareness inward.

Now, start to focus all your attention on your breathing. Release any thoughts in your mind by simply turning all your attention to your natural breathing rhythm.

Breathe in, breath out.

Feel the sensations in your chest as you breathe in and out and let your awareness only focus on these sensations.

As you continue to breathe in and out, you are releasing any tensions in your body. You are also releasing any pent-up emotions as you sink deeper and deeper into relaxation.

Simply enjoy your breathing and the feeling of calmness that is increasing with every inhale. You are relaxed. All the muscles in your body are soft and loose.

Now I want you to visualize yourself standing on top of the hill looking down onto a city or suburb.

It is autumn and as you stand on top of the hill you are in a cozy and warm jacket that is keeping you warm.

You are breathing in the cool crisp outdoor air and your mind feels refreshed and alert.

The is a gentle breeze caressing your face and you can smell the scent of ripe apples in this breeze.

You feel relaxed and at ease surrounded by the tranquility and vibrant energy of the beautiful nature all around you.

As you look down at the city down below let your imagination bring you the sights sounds and smells of this beautiful place.

As you breathe a little deeper start to walk down the hill towards the city down below. With every step you take closer to this city, the sounds and the colors get more pronounced.

You can see the colored rooftops, hear the bustle of the cars and the people in the city and you know that you want to get there as soon as possible.

As you walk down the path, there are a lot of beautiful scenes all around you, calling out to you and enticing you. However, even though you look around, you keep moving forward towards your destination without stopping.

You know where you want to go and you understand that the sooner you get there, the sooner you can settle in and start enjoying yourself.

With every step you take your destination gets closer and you can see it clearly. You are confident in your step because you can clearly see where you are going and you know what is waiting for you there.

A few more steps and you can hear the sound of laughter, cars and activity. You are drawn to the life within the city and although the nature surrounding you is beautiful; you know that your shelter lies in the city below.

As you draw nearer and nearer your step is getting lighter and you start to feel excited at the thought of reaching your destination.

Now at this moment, I want you to connect with that feeling of excitement and joy that you are feeling as you keep drawing closer and closer to your destination.

Doesn't it make you even more motivated to finish the journey? Does it not get easier the closer and closer you get to the city?

As you ask yourself these questions, let the answers come to you from deep down within. Let yourself come to the realization that the first step is the hardest part. After that, the action will be its own motivation and the rest of the steps will get easier.

Realize that everything you use to distract yourself and procrastinate is just like the beautiful scenery you are walking past as you walk down to the city. The scenery may be beautiful but come nightfall it will not offer you the shelter and security you need.

In this moment realize that your destination is only far if you are not moving towards it. Come to the realization that every step you take is one step closer to manifesting your dreams.

At this point, you are at the foot of the hill and you have made it to your destination. I want you to take a deep breath and tune into how you are feeling in this moment when you have reached the shelter of the city.

This feeling of safety and accomplishment is what you deny yourself every time you procrastinate. Let yourself experience it and feel what it feels like to get to your destination in time.

As you lean into this feeling I want you to internalize it and connect to it deeply. Tell yourself that you want to feel this sense of accomplishment and safety from now on.

You want to have the courage to keep moving towards your goals no matter what distractions are along this path.

Take a moment to connect with these realizations and commit them to your mind.

Every time you want to put off doing something or distract yourself, I want you to remember walking down the hill to the city below and how it feels to arrive at your destination.

Now take a deep breath in, and then exhale.

Feel yourself breathing in focus and motivation and letting go of any resistance to your purpose.

Take another deep breath in and as you exhale start to bring your awareness back to the present.

When you are ready, open your eyes.

This guided meditation is now complete.

Guided Meditations for Manifesting Good Grades 20 minutes

Duration 20 minutes.

Find a nice comfortable spot. You can close your eyes or leave them open.

Make sure you are sitting comfortably in an upright but relaxed posture. You can place your hands on your lap with the palm facing upward in a sign of openness to receiving and letting the universe guide you.

Let's start by getting centered and grounded in the present moment.

Breathe in deeply through the nose feeling the air fill your lungs completely then exhale slowly through the mouth.

Now repeat this deep breathing technique five more times. Deep inhale, slow exhale. Deep inhale, slow exhale. Deep inhale, slow exhale. Deep inhale, slow exhale. Now one last time, inhale deeply, then exhale slowly.

Now place your hand over your chest and allow yourself to feel the rhythm of your breathing as you allow your breathing to go back to normal.

Shut everything else out apart from the gentle rise and fall of your chest as you breathe in and out.

With every breath, you are going deeper and deeper into relaxation. Your mind is open and you feel a sense of clarity and calmness in your mind and body.

At this point I want you to think about your favorite thing in nature. Maybe it is majestic waterfalls, the beauty of a snowcapped mountain, the untamed beauty of wildlife or anything else that takes your breath away about nature.

When you find that thing that is most striking to you, I want you to now think of yourself as having the same magnificent energy of nature as the striking thing that came to your mind.

The same energy that fuels the water gushing down the waterfall is in you, lying dormant waiting for you to activate it. The same natural energy that fuels the volcanoes is available to you if only you will allow yourself to tap into it.

Whatever natural feature takes your breath away, I want you to come to the realization that the same energy that fuels it is also available to you from the universe.

You have limitless potential because the universe is ready to give you anything you need provided that you reach out and ask for it.

Nothing is out of reach for you because the powerful natural energy that fuels nature is also fueling your brain.

You are so powerful and capable of accomplishing anything you put your mind to because you have unlimited reserves of positive energy available to you from the universe.

Now I want you to take a deep breath and as you inhale, feel yourself inviting in radiant and powerful energy with every inhale.

As you continue to breathe in deeply, you are taking in more powerful energy and this energy is permeating every part of your being.

You feel your confidence grow with every exhale because you know that with this powerful energy from the universe, you can manifest the grades you want in any subject.

Nothing is too difficult for you. You have everything you need to take on any challenge and succeed.

Feel this power and confidence swell within you. Clear your mind of all self-imposed doubts and limiting beliefs.

Breathe in intelligence and confidence and as you exhale release any self-doubt.

Now I want you to visualize the grade you want to manifest. See it written clearly on your exam paper. As you look at that grade see your name written beside it. This is your grade.

How does it feel to see it on paper? Imagine yourself sitting at your desk with the paper marked A in your hand. How do you feel?

Now I want you to take this feeling and immerse yourself in it. The sense of accomplishment, the pride in passing, and the relief you feel at this moment. Take a moment to experience these feelings clearly and vividly.

With this mental picture in your mind, I want you to repeat these affirmations.

I am gifted.

I am intelligent.

Good grades come easily to me.

I learn fast and everything I learn I remember clearly.

I am attracting good grades right now.

I can accomplish anything I set my mind to.

The universe is fueling me with powerful energy to take on any challenge.

I am grateful for my intelligence.

I am grateful for my good grades.

As you affirm your intentions, I want you to connect with them deeply and let them resonate in your mind. Sit with them for a moment and let them penetrate your subconscious.

Now, gradually start to bring your awareness back to the present. Bring your awareness back to your body by tuning into the sensations of your breathing. Feel the air enter your body as you inhale and notice how your chest relaxes when you exhale.

When you are ready, you can open your eyes.

This guided meditation is now complete.

Manifest Your Life's Purpose - 10 minutes

If you want to manifest your life's purpose by resetting your mind, this meditation will help you attract your dharma and find your purpose.

Let's get started.

Duration:10 minutes

Start by getting comfortable. Sit in a quiet spot with your feet planted firmly on the ground.

Roll your shoulders slightly back to open up your chest> your back should be straight in an upright but relaxed posture.

Now close your eyes and let's start by getting you centered. To relax your mind and your body take a couple of deep breaths through your nose and then exhale slowly through your mouth.

One more time, breath in nice and deep, hold for a few seconds and then exhale.

Now let your breathing go back to its normal rhythm and allow yourself to sink deeper and deeper into relaxation.

Your whole body is relaxed and your mind is calm and receptive.

Now I want you to imagine that there is a glowing golden light at the top of your head.

This light is full of positive and peaceful energy that is now flowing into your body starting from the top of your head and flowing downwards all the way to your feet.

Allow this energy to calm your mind and relax your entire body as it continues to flow into every part of your body in warm gentle waves.

The more you are bathed in this energy the more relaxed and centered you feel.

Feel your body responding to this soothing energy. All your muscles are loose and soft. Your facial muscles are relaxed and your whole body feels energized and alive.

Now feel this cleansing energy start to dissipate all your stress and negative emotions. The more it courses through your body the more it frees you from negative thoughts and emotions.

You are covered in positivity and gentle soothing energy that has guided you to a peaceful and grounded state.

Now in this relaxed state, I want you to visualize yourself one year from now. Where do you see yourself? What are you doing? Who are you with?

As you visualize yourself at that point in the future, look around you. What do you have that you do not have now? How has your life changed? Are you content and happy where you are?

As you answer these questions, I want you to go back a little further into the future> Now you are five years into the future. Again, look around you and take in your surroundings. Where are you? What are you doing? Who are you with? Are you happy with what you see?

As you internalize the answers to these questions now let's go even deeper into the future. Now it's ten years from now, where do you see yourself? What has changed in your life? Who are you with? Are you fulfilled and content?

Now take all these three versions of yourself and in your mind hold them up side by side. You as you are now. You as you want to be in five years and you as you want to be in ten years.

As you compare these different stages of your life, ask yourself – what do I need to do now to get where I want to be in five years or ten?

Let this self-inquiry reveal to you your life purpose and the direction you need to steer your life in to manifest the outcome you want.

If you see yourself in a new home or at a better job in the future, what can you do now to manifest this reality? What steps can you take to attract the wealth, abundance and fulfillment you see in your future?

To manifest your purpose you need to create a link that aligns your intentions and actions today with the future that you want to create.

Sit with this realization for the moment and allow yourself to connect to the future versions of yourself that you want to manifest.

See yourself exactly as you want to be then. See the home that you want to be living in. See the car that you want to be driving. See the relationships that you want to have.

All these revelations will connect you with your purpose and connect you with your goals.

Now with this awareness, you can take a deep breath and bring your consciousness back to the present.

Take a series of deep breaths and exhales and feel yourself gradually return to the present.

When you are ready, you may open your eyes.

This guided mediation is now complete.

Chapter 10: A New Beginning

The power of affirmations in attracting the things you want is that they set a clear intention and purpose that seeps into your subconscious. If you want to change any sphere of your life, using affirmations to create the reality you want is one of the most effective ways to do it.

In this section, we shall focus on powerful affirmations that will help you create the future that you want.

Affirmations for Healthy Eating Habits - 10 minutes

You can repeat these affirmations daily to reset your mindset about food and manifest the body you want.

Duration 10 minutes:

In a quiet comfortable space, sit comfortably and bring your awareness inward by shutting out all external input.

To enhance clarity and open up your subconscious take a series of deep breaths until you feel calm and relaxed.

No in this relaxed state, close your eyes gently and repeat these affirmations.

I am attracted to healthy food.

I love to nurture and nourish my body.

I pay attention to how food makes me feel.

I respect my body and only feed it healthy and wholesome food.

I make healthy eating choices.

Healthy food makes me feel good.

Eating healthy is part of my lifestyle

I prefer healthy food over junk food

I eat to fuel my body

My body is a reflection of what I put in it.

I am grateful that my diet nourishes and keeps me healthy.

I choose healthy foods because they keep me strong and energized.

I choose healthy foods because my body is important to me.

I take care of my health by eating healthy.

I have a healthy relationship with food.

I feel great when I take care of myself.

I feel great when I eat right.

I manifest good health by eating healthy food.

Eating healthy comes easily to me.

Good food nourishes my body and my soul.

I make healthy eating choices.

I avoid any food that does not nourish my body.

I choose to be healthy.

I choose to eat right.

I choose to nourish my body.

After you affirm your intentions, take a deep breath and allow yourself to connect with these affirmations deeply. When you are ready you may open your eyes.

Affirmations for Manifesting Self Control and Discipline - 10 minutes

If your emotions often get the better of you, these affirmations will help you in staying calm and manifesting better self-regulation.

Duration: 10 minutes

Start by sitting comfortably with your feet planted firmly on the ground. Now take a few deep breaths to center yourself and direct all your awareness inward.

Now repeat these affirmations stating each clearly in your mind or speaking it softly out loud.

My self-control is growing stronger by the day.

Self-discipline comes naturally to me.

I have control over my impulses.

I am completely focused on succeeding.

I am committed to my goals.

I start each day with purpose and confidence.

I am in control of my habits.

I am in control of my emotions.

I do not make emotional decisions.

My mind is strong, capable, and disciplined.

I can tap into my willpower.

My choices are in agreement with my desires and my habits.

Every day my willpower becomes stronger.

I am in charge of my behavior and actions.

I exercise self-restraint.

I finish all tasks that I start.

I have the power to choose my thoughts and actions.

I am capable and I am disciplined.

I set and achieve goals effortlessly.

I align my actions with the outcomes I want to manifest.

Affirmations for Trusting the Universe to Manifest Your Desires - 10 minutes

Sometimes giving up the need for control can be the reset you need to attract the things you want to manifest. This short affirmation session will help you trust your journey and have faith that your desires will manifest.

Duration: 10 minutes

Recite these affirmations first thing in the morning before you start your day.

I am on the right path.

I am in alignment with my desires.

Everything always works out for me.

Everything is working out for me.

I will trust the universe to manifest my desires at the right time.

I do not need to always control the outcome.

I trust my journey.

I am manifesting the things I want right now.

I am exactly where I should be.

Everything I want is already available for me.

I am grateful for everything I already have.

My future is bright no matter what today looks like.

Nothing can block my abundance.

Nothing can block my wealth.

I trust the universe to provide me with all the things you need.

I can keep my focus on the present confident that my future is manifesting my desires.

I am free of anxiety and worry.

Every day I get closer to my dreams.

Morning Gratitude Affirmations - 10 minutes

Setting your day with gratitude is the best way to send out the right energy into the universe to manifest abundance and joy.

You can recite these affirmations daily first thing in the morning to reset your energy to gratitude and appreciation.

Duration: 10 minutes

You can repeat these affirmations while seated in a comfortable chair. To really connect with your subconscious, close your eyes and focus all your attention inward.

When you feel calm and centered, repeat these affirmations slowly and with clarity.

I am grateful to be alive.

I am grateful to this day.

I am grateful for the abundance I create.

I am grateful for the prosperity I attract.

I am grateful for the people in my life.

I am grateful for the riches that flow into my life.

I am grateful for the presence of love in my life.

I am grateful for where I am right now.

I am grateful for all I have experienced in my life.

I am grateful for the amazing potential the future holds.

I am grateful for this moment right here, right now.

I am grateful for everyone who loves me.

I am grateful for everyone who challenges me.

I am grateful for the wonders of mother nature.

I am grateful for plants and animals.

I am grateful for the wind and the weather.

I am grateful for all my skills and talents.

I am grateful for endless opportunities.

I am grateful for the full range of emotions I feel.

I am grateful for the things that excite me.

I am grateful for the many things that bring me joy.

I am grateful for this day, teeming with potential.

I am grateful for another opportunity to serve and live life to the fullest.

I am grateful for being a beneficial presence on the planet.

I am grateful for all that I have.

When you finish the recitations take a moment to sit with your intentions and commit them to your mind. You may now open your eyes.

Total Hours - 11

Conclusion

The power of the universe is infinite. Every day we are surrounded by miracles and the giving nature of the universe. All you have to do to tap into this infinite reservoir of abundance, wealth, and joy is to align your inner energy with that of the universe. This means being aware of your subconscious beliefs, values, and intentions. Unfortunately, the subconscious exists just below the surface of your consciousness. Even when you are not aware of it, it is directing your thoughts, habits, and actions.

To tap into this subconscious layer of your mind that determines the energy you project into the universe, it is important to become more mindful and in touch with your inner self. This is why meditation is one of the most effective tools you can use to attract and manifest wealth, abundance, love and everything else you yearn for. Meditation does not just show you how to tap into your subconscious but it also allows you to reset your subconscious to project energy that is in alignment with the goals you want to manifest.

Throughout this book, we have equipped you with the tools you need to manifest the outcomes you want in different spheres of your life. With these meditation tools, you can harness the law of attraction to create the reality that you want to live in. If your subconscious energy is not aligned with the things you want to manifest, the law of attraction cannot work for you.

Now that we have shown you exactly how you can reset your subconscious energy to start manifesting everything you have always wanted, all you need to do is find a comfortable space and start meditating. Meditation is one of the most powerful mind control tools that will help you project the right energy into the universe. once you are in control of your subconscious energy then everything you need to manifest is right within your control.

We hope this book helps you to manifest your deepest desires using the principle of the law of attraction. You now have all the tools you need to create the life you have always wanted so all you need to do is get started.